HUMAN BEHAVIOR

FROM A SPIRITUAL PERSPECTIVE

SPIRITUAL DEVELOPMENT BEGINS IN YOUR MIND

HOW TO ACHIEVE SUCCESS GOD'S WAY

BOOK 2
MENTAL TOOLS

BY

DWAYNE D. WILLIAMS

HUMAN BEHAVIOR

FROM A SPIRITUAL PERSPECTIVE

Spiritual Development Begins in Your Mind

How to Achieve Success God's Way

BY

DWAYNE D. WILLIAMS

Human Behavior from a Spiritual Perspective:
Spiritual Development Begins in Your Mind
How to Achieve Success God's Way—Book 2
Copyright © 2017 by Dwayne D. Williams
ISBN: 978-0-9847157-8-7
www.tier1education.com
www.dwaynedwilliams.com
Email: dwayne@tier1education.com
Twitter information: @dwaynedwilliams
Facebook: https://www.facebook.com/dwaynedwilliams1

Editors: Geoff Fuller and Dianna Palumbo
Typesetter: Dan Yeager, Nu-Image Design
Book cover designer: Dan Yeager, Nu-Image Design

Pronouns that are capitalized within Scripture quotations identify God.

"All personal achievement starts in the mind of the individual. Your personal achievement starts in your mind. The first step is to know exactly what your problem, goal, or desire is."

~W Clement Stone

CONTENTS

Acknowledgements

I thank God for giving me the inspiration and passion to write for countless hours about the role our minds play in spiritual development and how to use faith to access the blessings of God. I am thankful for the many people who have impacted my life, including my parents, siblings, spiritual leaders, and mentors. I thank my wife, Toni Williams, and children, Dwayne D. Williams and Noni D. Williams, for their continual love and encouragement. I also thank Dan Yeager, Geoff Fuller, and Dianne Palumbo for their attention to this work.

About the Author

Dwayne D. Williams is becoming the most sought after success coach within the education community. He is most known for his work as a school psychologist, in which he helps teachers, administrators, and state departments create educational models and instructional strategies that increase performance among students of color.

Dwayne has been a believer in Christ for over 25 years. As a certified success coach, Dwayne integrates psychological principles and Scripture to help clients develop their gifts, talents, and abilities—and to achieve success God's way, according to Scripture.

Dwayne earned a master's degree (M.A.) in psychology and an Educational Specialist degree (Ed.S.) from Marshall University Graduate College. He earned a bachelor's degree (B.A.) in psychology from Fairmont State University and an associate's degree (A.A.) from William Rainey Harper College. Dwayne received training in the area of life coaching/ success coaching with Youth and Family Guidance Incorporated and received board-certified life coaching credentials through the Center for Credentialing and Education (CCE).

Dwayne is the CEO of Tier 1 Educational Coaching and Consulting Firm, an educational organization that helps administrators, educators, parents, and community leaders create programs and models that are culturally responsive, models that increase performance among culturally diverse students, including African American students. Dwayne is married to Toni Williams, and they have two beautiful children—Dwayne II and Noni Williams.

INTRODUCTION

If you read book 1 of this series, you learned that the first edition of *Human Behavior from a Spiritual Perspective* focused solely on understanding Christ's work at the cross and understanding how to use your mind to develop spiritually. The second edition of this work starts the "Human Behavior from a Spiritual Perspective Series," which comprises 2 books.

This book, *Mental Tools*, is book 2 of the series; it focuses on how to use your mind to develop spiritually and to achieve success in every area of your life. Mental tools refer to mental abilities, including thinking, reasoning, meditating, memorizing, and learning.

I strongly encourage you to read book 1 before you read this book. Self-Concepts, which is the theme of book 1, focuses on the importance of becoming aware of yourself, including your strengths, your weaknesses, your fears, your hopes, and your desires. Book 1 addresses who you are as an earthly and spiritual person. *Mental Tools* will help you address the following questions:

- What mental tools must I use to develop my thinking according to God's Word?
- What kind of thoughts must I produce to create the habits of God?
- Why must I create "mental warning signs" in order to develop spiritually and to access the blessings of God?
- Why does God place great emphasis on learning "accurate" information?
- Why is meditation a powerful mental tool?
- What does the Bible say about weaknesses and how can I turn my weaknesses into strengths?
- What is the purpose of memory in spiritual development?
- What does it mean to have the mind of Christ?

- What must I do to eliminate the "three-letter-phrase" from my mind that causes me to doubt and prolong my calling?

This book will help you use your mind to create a more meaningful and successful life. After reading Books 1 and 2 in order, you will gain the self-awareness skills needed to declare victory in your life. You will know exactly how to use mental tools, such as learning, memory, faith, meditation, and other mental attributes and live the life that God predestined for you!

WHAT'S IN THIS BOOK?

This book includes 7 chapters. Chapters 1-4 focus on the importance of renewing your mind. These four chapters focus specifically on why you must renew your mind to develop spiritually and to achieve the blessings that God has for you. When I provide success coaching to clients, I explain that it is important that we understand, from a spiritual perspective, why certain things happen in life as they do. It is also important that we understand why we may create and harbor negative thoughts about our worth, about our skills, about other people, and about life. God did not create us with a mind that produces negative thoughts about our worth, our abilities, and ourselves. Thus, the first step in understanding human behavior from a spiritual perspective and achieving success God's way is understanding how and why our minds have been rewired to produce thoughts that work against our success. As the old adage goes, "The first step in defeating our enemy is understanding who our enemy is." The first four chapters of this book expose our enemy.

Chapters 5-7 focus on the importance of understanding yourself and how you have become the person you are at this very moment. To develop spiritually and to experience success in every area of our lives, it is vital that we become self aware and understand how we have become the person we are this very moment. Chapters 5-7 reveals how you have become the person you are today, from a spiritual perspective, and will steer you in the direction to change your outlook on yourself. As I explain to the professionals whom I coach, in order to identify your purpose in life, in order to develop spiritually, and in order to experience success God's way, you must begin with yourself!

CHAPTER ONE:
SANCTIFYING YOUR MIND

For I delight in the law of God according to the inward man.
But I see another law in my members, warring against the law
of my mind, and bringing me into captivity to the law of sin,
which is in my members. O wretched man that I am! Who will
deliver me from this body of death? I thank God—through
Jesus Christ our Lord! So then, with the mind I myself serve the
law of God, but with the flesh the law of sin.

Romans 7:22-25, NKJV

For the next few seconds, think about people you know who were on fire for God but at some time in their life, lost their zeal for the Lord and began to live a lifestyle characterized by drinking, smoking, and ungodly behaviors. Bring these individuals to your mind. Who were they? What do you believe was the single greatest reason these people reverted to a lifestyle of ungodly behaviors?

When I reflect on these questions, a 30-year-old man comes to mind. For the sake of this story, I will call him Minister John Doe. Minister Doe began preaching in his mid 20s. As a child, whenever I saw him in the community, he had his Bible with him. And carrying his Bible was not for show; he had a genuine passion and zeal for the Word of God. Minister Doe had a particular shine to him that words cannot describe. People often explained that his face glowed with passion for the Lord.

I loved getting up early on Sunday morning, because I knew Minister Doe taught Sunday School. As a young boy, I thought Minister Doe had a certain type of swagger to him; I found him to be cool, calm, and collected, unlike many of the traditional preachers who "hooped" and "hopped" around the church while teaching the Word.

Although Minister Doe touched the lives of many, he eventually began to drink liquor and smoke cigarettes. When the believers asked him about these behaviors, to encourage him to quit, he denied that he engaged in smoking cigarettes and drinking alcohol. More people began to question the behaviors of Minister Doe, and eventually he began to miss Sunday morning services. Gradually, Minister Doe quit coming to church and began to engage in drinking and smoking behaviors publically, without shame. Minister Doe became comfortable with entering public places tipsy and sloppy drunk at times. When he was drunk, he often quoted Scriptures and talked about God.

After speaking with Minister Doe, I learned that he experimented with drinking and smoking activities privately, within his home, although he continued to attend church and preached the gospel. He engaged in these behaviors for a prolonged period and these behaviors became habits; he began to desire these behaviors upon awaking in the morning. Interestingly, Minister Doe used his own life and experiences to shed light on how people of God could be distracted from their calling and purpose by creating habits that are ungodly.

Many people believe developing spiritually is difficult, but the problem lies in their minds. Like Minister Doe, many people engage in ungodly behaviors repeatedly and create habits that separate them from God's glory. Spiritual development requires that we activate faith, learn godly principles, and live according to His Word, while separating ourselves from lifestyles that may interfere with our development. The key to developing spiritually is engaging in habits that will allow God to sanctify our minds. When God sanctifies our minds, we eventually produce behaviors that align with His Word.

SANCTIFICATION AND HOLINESS

The Bible speaks about *sanctification* and *holiness*, but what do these terms mean? Sanctification and holiness are similar in meaning. They both refer to the state of being cleansed and set apart for sacred use.

When I was a child, I often heard people state, while giving their testimony, "I'm saved, sanctified, and filled with the Holy Ghost!" I never knew what these expressions meant, although I enjoyed watching people shout around the church as they proclaimed their sanctification and holiness. Testimony service was always the best part of the service for me. It was always very emotional and animated.

Prior to entering church, my mother often warned me not to stare at people or smile as they rejoiced around the sanctuary. As we pulled into the church parking lot, she would usually remind me about how I should act during service: "All right, Dwayne, you best not be in here playing and staring at people when they shout. You better get in here and act like you got some sense!" Her statement is not what motivated me to act right; it was always the look on her face that kept me in check. As a child, I thought going to church for many years, praying, and reading God's Word lead to sanctification. I wasn't completely wrong, but I definitely missed the most important factor, which is the work of Jesus Christ.

Many people have false perceptions about the process of sanctification. They accept Christ in their lives and believe they don't have to do anything else to develop spiritually because they confessed, "Yes, I believe. I believe Jesus died for my sins!" From their confession, they believe God will send a tornado in their lives that will destroy and remove everything that is unlike Him. They believe their emotions for people will change immediately and that they will acquire agape love at the time of their confession. Unfortunately, this is not always the case.

Others often doubt their salvation because after having confessed Christ as their Savior, they eventually engaged in the exact things they had asked God to deliver them from. From these experiences, they not only doubted their salvation, but also the existence of God. If this has happened to you, you should realize that I don't know anyone who has made drastic changes in their life the very moment they confessed Christ as their Savior.

I'm sure there are many people who were set free from addictions and delivered from sinful habits the moment they confessed Christ as their Savior. But most people I know have told me it was a process for them, and I must say it definitely was a process for me. In fact, I went back and forth with my lifestyle for years. I wasn't delivered until I started understanding the person of Christ, and it should go without saying that there are things from which I still seek deliverance! I should also say that I went back and forth with my lifestyle only because I did not submit to God's Word.

My point is God works with us in different ways, based on our faith—our belief that He can and will align our thoughts with His. This is what faith is all about. If you maintain a sinful lifestyle and produce thoughts that are contrary to God's Word, you must believe that God can and will renew your mind.

THE PROCESS OF SANCTIFICATION

Sanctification is a process that begins with accepting Christ as our personal Savior, which entails believing in His work at the cross. When most believers speak of sanctification, they refer to their lifestyles and being set apart from old, sinful habits. Many believe they do not experience sanctification until they are able to refrain from certain negative behaviors. But this is not what the Bible says. Actually, the moment you accept Christ into your life, God sanctifies you.

> *"Sacrifice and offerings, burnt offerings, and offerings for sin you did not desire, nor had pleasure in them" (which are offered according to the law), then He said, "Behold, I have come to do Your will, O God." He takes away the first [law] that He may establish the second. By that will we have been sanctified through the offering of the body of Jesus Christ once for all.*

> Hebrews 10:8-10, NKJV

The above text shows us that when we accept the offering of the body of Christ—dying on the cross—we immediately experience sanctification from death to life. From our acceptance, God immerses us in His blood, and removes us from a state of condemnation. This removal from darkness and condemnation to light is what we call redemption (Ephesians 1:7-8). The fact that Christ redeemed you from the death of sin means you have experienced sanctification in the spiritual realm. This is true no matter what you felt at the time of your confession. Therefore, when you accepted Christ into your life, you actually accepted His offer to remove you from darkness (separation from God) into His marvelous light (God's presence). You have salvation because the blood of God has sanctified you!

But we are bound to give thanks to God always for you, brethren beloved by the Lord, because God from the beginning chose you for salvation through sanctification by the Spirit and belief in the truth.

II Thessalonians 2:13 NKJV

When we accept Christ into our lives, we actually give Him permission to renew our minds. Believing in the works of Christ is vital in that if it were not for His experiences at the cross, sanctification would be impossible. The reason is clear: Everything that embodies sanctification comes from the blood of Christ, the Lamb of God!

In I Thessalonians, Paul prayed that the believers would be sanctified in all aspects of their lives—including their thinking, actions, desires, and habits. He prayed that God would sanctify their entire being, their spirit, soul, and body.

Now may the God of peace Himself sanctify you completely; and may your whole spirit, soul, and body be preserved blameless at the coming of our Lord Jesus Christ. He who calls you is faithful, who also will do it.

I Thessalonians 5:23-24, NKJV

The apostle Paul gave the believers at the church of Thessalonica hope. His message was clear: Develop spiritually, and in the process, allow God to sanctify you completely. It's important to realize that these believers had to open their minds and embrace the word preached in order for God to sanctify them completely. Paul's message to the church of Thessalonica exemplifies the *second* process of sanctification. It involves allowing God to sanctify us completely by working effectively on our minds, a process of allowing God to separate us from old, sinful habits.

Sanctifying us completely does not indicate that we will reach a certain hierarchy of sanctification, a level that is higher than other believers in Christ. Rather, it involves maturing in all aspects of life. Maturation in this sense refers to spiritual, mental, and emotional development; it involves learning to apply the work of Christ to our entire being and allowing the Spirit of God to separate us from activities and behaviors that are unlike Him.

This is an ongoing process in that we will never arrive at a perfect state in our lives. But we will eventually arrive at a place where we can separate ourselves from the pattern of this world. And as Paul declared, He who called us is faithful; He will do it. In other words, Christ will separate us from the things that hinder our development—the very things that we believe are impossible to defeat with our own abilities.

The second part of sanctification—which is allowing God to work effectively on our minds—is more demanding than simply accepting Christ into our lives, for it requires that we fill our minds with His Word and live by faith. John 15:7 says, "If you remain in Me [Christ] and My words remain in you, ask whatever you wish, and it will be given you."

Remaining in His words simply means living through Christ, by faith. We mature in Christ when we continue to believe what God has promised. For example, everything that is written in the Bible is to mature us. But it is through faith that we believe the information and experience sanctification. Think about this for a moment. If we do not activate our faith, our reading of His Word is simply that, just reading.

The Bible was written to inspire faith in God and to reveal to us spiritual principles that are unknown to the natural mind. The Word provides examples of people who lived by faith and shows how these people matured, as they believed God's Word. When we come to the decision that we will activate our faith, we rely less on human abilities and focus more on His Word; we allow the voice of God—His Word—to speak to our hearts and we respond to Him through faith.

Hebrews chapter 11 describes faith-based lifestyles. It explains, "By faith Abel offered God a better sacrifice than Cain did" (Hebrews 11:4). "By faith Enoch was taken from this life, so that he did not experience death" (Hebrews 11:5). "By faith Noah, when warned about things not yet seen, in holy fear built an ark to save his family. By his faith he condemned the world and became heir of the righteousness that comes by faith" (Hebrews 11:7). "By faith Abraham, when called to go to a place he would later receive as his inheritance, obeyed and went, even though he did not know where he was going" (Hebrews 11:8). "By faith Abraham, even though he was past age—and Sarah herself was barren—was enabled to become a father because he considered him faithful who had made the promise" (Hebrews 11:11). "By faith, Abraham, when God tested him, offered Isaac as a sacrifice" (Hebrews 11:17). "By faith Isaac blessed Jacob and Esau in regard to their future" (Hebrews 11:20). "By faith Joseph, when his end was near, spoke about the exodus of the Israelites from Egypt and gave instructions about his bones" (Hebrews 11:22).

As mentioned, sanctification is the process of separating ourselves, a process of reserving ourselves for sacred use. It is impossible to separate ourselves from old habits and sinful behaviors using natural abilities alone. Christ died so that we can experience sanctification and holiness. His Word leads us through this process. Thus, sanctification is a process we experience when we accept Christ into our lives and is an ongoing process by which we allow the Spirit to cleanse our minds from old thought patterns and sinful behaviors. The Bible says when we renew our minds we are a new creation, the old has gone and the new has come (II Corinthians 5:17). This is actually a statement of faith. Our statement of faith comes to fruition as we allow the Word of God to work effectively with our minds.

The process of sanctification explains why sinful desires and habits often do not cease immediately upon accepting Christ. Rather, they usually remain a part of our lives until God's Word cleanses our minds. For example, you may know someone who dedicated their life to God, but continues to demonstrate behaviors that are contrary to His will. When

I gave my life to God years ago, I continued in habits that characterized sin and shame. I began to demonstrate behaviors that characterize love, joy, peace, gentleness, and self-control only after I submitted my mind to the will and Word of God. Also, after submitting my mind, I noticed an increase in creative thinking and my purpose became clearer. By submitting, I allowed God to sanctify my mind. I began to think positively even in the midst of chaos and stress from this process. This transition in how my mind functioned—increased creativity and positive thoughts—was not produced from my natural ability. It was not a result of reading psychology books, meeting with a success coach, or meeting with a psychologist or therapist. Rather, my increase was supernatural in that the Spirit of God began to activate positive thoughts and novel ideas within my mind, ideas that enabled me to create and produce. Stated differently, I began to operate from the mind of Christ.

My story of transition explains why many believers have accepted Christ as their Savior, but their minds remain full of sinful habits and desires. These believers continue with their sinful lifestyles because they have accepted Christ as their Savior, but have not allowed Him to work on their minds. Christ washed them in His blood, upon their confession, but they have not allowed His Word to renew their thoughts.

Sanctification, then, is a process that matures us daily. Realize that the initial part of sanctification is not a process; for Romans chapter 10, verse 9 says, "That if you confess with your mouth, 'Jesus is Lord,' and believe in your heart that God raised Him from the dead, you will be saved." Maturation actually starts when we allow our minds to become susceptible to godly habits. We become susceptible to godly habits by abiding in Christ, which means activating faith in His Word.

HABITS AND SANCTIFICATION

Although sanctification happens internally, we are able to identify its fruits through human behaviors; we are able to identify Christ in our lives through habits. Most people are familiar with habits, but many do not realize the impact habits have on their earthly and spiritual lives. For example, habits are responsible for

- creating relationships,
- destroying relationships,
- developing spiritually,
- living through faith,
- doubting God,
- offending people,
- fornicating,
- displaying love,
- engaging in lustful thinking,
- committing adultery.

And the list goes on. Actually, the list is endless! Habits are behavioral patterns that we learn from engaging in the same behaviors repeatedly. When we engage in behaviors for a prolonged period, our mind performs the behaviors for us, without our awareness. This is a powerful mental ability.

Many people have a difficult time developing spiritually because their actions are rooted in sinful habits, which means they have overengaged in sinful activities. Consequently, their minds automatically produce ungodly thoughts, and their physical actions reflect their ungodly thinking. Since most people are familiar with the first part of sanctification, which is accepting Christ as our Savior, I will focus on the second part, which is cleansing our mind through habits.

Sanctifying our minds is both a natural and spiritual phenomena. It is natural because it deals with the earthly mind and mental abilities— I'll call this the *process*. It is spiritual because it deals with the person of Christ, His Spirit—I'll call this the *content*. The content deals with actual behaviors that we make habitual, which come from the Word of God. To understand how our minds create habits, I will explain this process using earthly behaviors. In the next chapter, I will explain, step by step, how to use this ability to create godly habits.

CAN WE AVOID HABITS?

Because God designed our minds to memorize behaviors that we produce most frequently, habits are unavoidable. Typically, behaviors that we demonstrate daily are the ones that become habits.

We create habits from stimulus-response interactions. A stimulus is *anything* we can sense within our world, anything we can see, hear, taste, touch, or smell. It is information that we sense from our environments. Stated differently, a stimulus is anything we can respond to. For example, we respond to the weather. If it is cold outdoors, we usually prepare for the coldness by covering our bodies with thick layers of clothing, including coats, hats, boots, and gloves. If it is hot outdoors, we usually respond by wearing clothing that will make us most comfortable.

If we wear hats, boots, sweaters, and coats in 90° weather, there is a good chance that we will experience a heat stroke. Because of our bodily systems, we usually respond appropriately to hot and cold weather. For example, our bodies sweat when we are hot in an attempt to cool us, and our bodies shiver when we are cold in an attempt to warm us. We put on and take off clothing based on these responses. In these examples, the stimulus is the *temperature* of the weather. We respond to the weather based on how the temperature makes us feel.

I'll use fire as another example. If we touch fire with our hands, we automatically jerk our hands back; it is usually an instant reaction. The fire is the stimulus to which we respond. Now think about music. When we turn on the radio, if the music is unpleasant, we usually turn the station until we find something more pleasant to our minds and spirits. We may even pop in a CD if we believe the radio station is playing too many commercials. Music and commercials are the *stimuli* (plural of *stimulus*) in these examples. From the examples, you should realize that the Bible is also a stimulus. Either we respond to God's voice (stimulus) by walking in faith, in an attempt to develop spiritually, or we respond by rejecting His Word, in an attempt to close His mouth.

Essentially, our senses present our minds with information from our environments. We respond to the information favorably or unfavorably. If the stimulus or environmental information is favorable, that is, if it gratifies us, we'll learn to desire it: If putting on a coat and hat gratifies our bodies when the weather is cold, we will desire a coat and hat the next time it is cold outdoors. If the stimulus produces an unfavorable response, if it does not lead to pleasure or a sense of fulfilled need, chances are, we will ignore or avoid it in the future: Because we realize that we would sweat profusely if we wore layers of clothing in 90° weather, we usually avoid sweaters, coats, and hats during the summer. These are our responses to the weather.

We create habits out of these behaviors because we engage in them often. I live in the Chicago area. When most people I know go outdoors during the winter season, they grab their coats without thinking. They rarely run outdoors and say, "Oh, I forgot to get my coat!"

Habits begin with the conscious mind, with which we direct our attention and awareness to a limited amount of information within our environments. We usually direct our attention to information that will gratify us or fulfill our immediate or future needs. Once we find the things that gratify us, we tend to *overengage* in the behaviors. When we produce the same response to a particular stimulus for a prolonged period, our mind memorizes the response and performs that behavior—in the presence of the stimulus—automatically. We do not have to think about performing the behavior because our minds engage in the behavior without our conscious thinking.

THE HABITS OF SMOKING AND DRINKING

To gain a better understanding of developing habits, consider the examples of smoking cigarettes and drinking alcoholic beverages. Most people who are addicted to smoking cigarettes and drinking alcohol were not born with these addictions (although some people are more prone to these addictions from birth). Rather, some time in their lives, people who smoke or drink were presented with a cigarette or an alcoholic beverage.

Simply having possession of a cigarette or an alcoholic beverage did not determine their drinking or smoking habit. Rather, at some point, they enjoyed the pleasure that came with the cigarette or beverage. From their pleasure, the gratification, they began to desire the stimulus. It's important to note, however, that the desire was not the physical stimulus, which in my example was the cigarette and the beverage. Rather, it was the sensation they experienced from the stimulus. Because of their desire to feel good or to fulfill a need, they responded to the stimulus in the same manner over a prolonged period. They responded by smoking the cigarette or drinking the beverage, and over time, their mind memorized the effect—the pleasure—and the person began to desire that cigarette or beverage.

The memory for the stimulus is so strong, for many individuals, that they can often taste the stimulus even when they do not have access to it. The need to gain a sensation and to feel good explains why people, before they have created the habit, will drink alcohol although it has a toxic taste. From drinking continuously, they acquire a taste for what had been distasteful.

In the above example, I used cigarettes and alcohol, but we create habits out of just about anything: from setting our keys on the table to the way with which we hold the steering wheel while driving our vehicles. The underlying factor is, through repetition, our minds memorize behaviors, and consequently, we act habitually.

THE SUBCONSCIOUS MIND: MAINTAINING HABITS

The most influential factor that hinders our ability to create the habits of God is not our conscious awareness, as many people believe. Rather, *subconscious* processes of our minds are most influential. Subconscious processes are mental activities that work outside our conscious awareness. To illustrate subconscious mental activities, I'll describe, on a very basic level, your reading of this book.

When you picked this book up, your eyes began to scan the print automatically, as you read the title and flipped through the pages. Your reading was automatic. Instead of focusing on individual letters and individual sounds, your mind crunched the letters and sounds together to produce words. Your ability to crunch the letters together automatically, and read them fluently, is a result of your subconscious mind.

Because you have read print for a *prolonged period,* when your eyes connect with letters and words you are familiar with, your mind automatically interprets the print. This is what we call reading. Your subconscious mind does it for you without your conscious effort. This would not be the case if you were to come across a word with which you are unfamiliar.

If you were to come across an unfamiliar word, you would have to *consciously* sound the word out. Your sounding each letter out would be your conscious effort. To make this point clear, read the following word: *Telangiectasia*. *Telangiectasia* is a medical term. Chances are, you had to consciously sound this word out, because you may not be used to seeing or hearing it. Medical students who study telangiectasia would probably read it fluently, upon sight.

It may sound a bit inaccurate to say that subconscious processes are responsible for maintaining habits given that our conscious awareness is responsible for creating them. After all, we would have to consciously select behaviors to create them, right? Right! But without subconscious activities, behaviors that are repeated will not develop into habits. Habits develop because our subconscious minds produce behaviors without our conscious awareness. In other words, we act without thinking about our actions because subconscious activities perform behaviors for us automatically.

We all have either said, "Wow, maybe I shouldn't have said that," or thought, "I didn't mean to say it that way. It just came out." We usually make the latter remarks when we automatically say negative comments that are on our minds. We speak without considering the potential damage our words may impose on other people's attitude or mood.

I have created a habit of grabbing my keys and then leaving out the door for work. When I think I'm ready to leave for work, my mind automatically directs me to my keys. I could have an array of things on my mind, things that I have to complete for the day. In the midst of my thinking about my assignments for the day, I would be walking out the door and preparing to start my car, without having thought about grabbing my keys. Now that I have identified this habit, I set my lunch and other items by my keys. This practice allows me to see these items prior to grabbing my keys and leaving.

Psychologists call the process of demonstrating behaviors without thinking *automatization*. This big word simply means *automatic processing*. When behaviors become automatic, we no longer need conscious awareness to control them. Rather, habitual behaviors control us. Through repetition, our minds will have memorized the behaviors [habits] and will produce them in the presence of the stimuli (things/items) that once controlled them.

Remember, we create habits from stimulus-response interactions. When people who now have smoking habits were presented cigarettes (stimulus), they responded by smoking them (response). Their subconscious minds will now respond to the stimulus in the same way, without their conscious help: That is, they'll pick up matches or lighters, light their cigarette and smoke it without thinking about smoking. Before creating the habit, they premeditated on smoking: They thought about smoking before actually doing it; also, they thought about smoking as they did it. Most often, they thought about the way the cigarette made them feel.

After creating the habit, they'd smoke, subconsciously, with other things on their mind. In some cases, some people's smoking habit is so strong that they'll light a cigarette and finish smoking it before remembering they lit one! This process will control all behaviors that have become habits. All that is needed is the stimulus that once created the habit.

SINFUL HABITS?

We also create sinful habits from stimulus-response interactions. For example, if you constantly engaged in lustful thought patterns when you observed an attractive male or female, your subconscious mind will automatically place you into a lustful state of mind when attractive men or women are in your presence, even without your conscious awareness. We rarely consider lustful thought patterns as habits because they are mental, but we form all sorts of mental habits.

People usually overlook small habits such as mental thoughts, lying, or showing favoritism. Since people, including believers, often overengage in these behaviors for a prolonged period, these same behaviors are stored into their subconscious minds. Consequently, these people demonstrate behaviors such as lying and showing favoritism habitually.

One common mental habit is the tendency to think negatively about others. For those who have created habits of thinking negatively about others, their subconscious minds generate negative thoughts automatically in the presence of certain people. For example, the moment they encounter the individual they perceive negatively, whether the encounter is in the form of a picture, idea, or actual person, the individual that has the mental habit generates negative thoughts automatically. And in most cases, the person with the mental habit is not aware of their negative thoughts. They demonstrate these negative behaviors unknowingly!

Although we create them like other habits, sinful habits are most difficult to reverse. You may ask, "What are sinful habits?" The answer is any thought or behavior that is contrary to God's Word. These may include the following behaviors: envy, covetousness, wickedness, perversion, lying, fornication, adultery, hatred, showing favoritism, backbiting, and other behaviors revealed in Romans 1:28-32.

We have a tendency to direct our attention toward sinful activities and respond to them, over time, with repetition. From creating sinful habits, our bodies begin to desire sin. But something happens to us when we create sinful habits, something more spiritual. From sinning continuously, our minds and spirits become the property of sin.

Our *bodies,* the physical property of our spirits, become the physical property of sin. In other words, we become slaves to sin. Remember, Christ has made sin powerless. Because of His work at the cross, sin does not have dominion over our minds when we live through Christ. But when we create sinful habits and lifestyles, we provide sin the power to control our minds through habits. As such, sin commands our minds and spirits to gratify our bodies. Sin's power and rule over our minds and spirits make it difficult to reverse sinful habits. Even when we greatly desire to reverse these habits, it is extremely difficult.

RETURNING TO THE OLD COVENANT LAW

Many of us attempt to free ourselves from sinful habits and negative thinking by using self-effort and human reasoning. We often desire professional advice, but fail to seek God for our deliverance. When we attempt to conquer our addictions, fears, and habits using human ability and intelligence alone, we commit ourselves to the old covenant law.

The old law was based on works: It was based on the Israelites' ability to accomplish things using human effort. The old law was also a covenant that exposed the Israelites' *inability* to free themselves from negative thinking and ungodly habits. Thus, by attempting to free ourselves from sinful habits using human effort and human intellect, we put faith in the old law. We attempt to become righteous by using human powers.

Many of us find difficulty breaking sinful habits because, although we are living in the covenant of grace, we attempt to free ourselves from addictions and sinful habits using our minds, apart from Christ. When we attempt to free ourselves from sinful habits, the old covenant reveals the difficulty in accomplishing such an impossible feat. This concept is extremely important.

I've counseled people who have said that they've met with their advisors, spoken with people they trust, and have tried many interventions, but still experience depression. Some have admitted that they had felt the only answer to their problem was suicide. The reason for their desire to take their lives is spiritual. Allow me to explain.

When we commit ourselves to the old covenant law, the law does what it was created to do: It not only exposes sin but also our inability to deliver ourselves from sinful thinking and living. It exposes the difficulty in breaking habits using human effort and shows clearly that we need Christ to intervene on our behalf. In his book, *Unmerited Favor,* Pastor Joseph Prince describes this concept best. Pastor Prince explained that the old covenant works similar to how a mirror works: If you look in a mirror, the mirror will reveal your appearance. If you have dirt on your face, the mirror will reveal the dirt; if you have a scratch on your face, the mirror will reveal the scratch. Essentially, the mirror allows you to see your imperfections. Likewise, when we commit ourselves to the old covenant by attempting to work for our deliverance, the law works as a mirror—it not only shows us our sins and flaws, but also how impossible it is for us to deliver ourselves from negative thinking and living.

Earlier, I mentioned that people have told me they have contemplated suicide because of their inability to free themselves from depressive thoughts. From a spiritual perspective, these people have thought about ending their lives because the old covenant tormented them. As the law showed them how impossible it was for them to deliver themselves, these people lost hope, felt like throwing in the towel, and believed suicide was the only way out.

I'll make this more concrete. Think about what happens to the person who is struggling with an issue or habit that she feels is impossible to break. Because the person desires to be free, she may consult with her pastor, relative, physician, therapist, and psychologist. Usually, when most mental health professionals speak with people about breaking habits, they give earthly advice; they refer to "scientifically based interventions." Mental health professionals usually tell clients to try hard, use mental strategies, think positively, attempt to think about their thoughts, and avoid certain people and certain environments.

What we fail to acknowledge, however, when giving advice and recommendations concerning breaking habits is this: If we focus on human effort alone to experience deliverance, we actually encourage people to return to the old covenant. We encourage them to attempt to defeat their issues using their own abilities. Usually, people experience depression because the law shows their inability to free their minds.

The law recalls all human interventions the individual has tried. The law not only recalls human interventions, but also sheds light on how ineffective they were. Remember, the law works like a mirror. Because the person *sees* how impossible it is to become free and believes there is nothing she could do to feel better, she loses hope and desires suicide. What is worse than simply having a habit or issue is wanting to be delivered from the habit, but feeling that deliverance is impossible. For example, many people have addictions and negative habits, but they enjoy their habits and do not desire deliverance. Others have addictions and negative habits, but desire change. They see where they want to be in life, but feel that because of their habit or inability to free their minds, they will never reach their true potential. People usually lose hope when they can see their deliverance—they see their potential—but also see the impossibility of freeing themselves.

It is important to note, however, that because of Christ's work at the cross, we do not have to depend solely on ourselves and on human interventions for deliverance. Rather, we can depend on Christ and His work at the cross for our breakthrough. We return to the old law when we do not make Christ central to our intervention. That is, we operate under the old law when we exclude God and attempt to use our own ability to deliver ourselves.

Many people have made habits of using self-effort to defeat negative thinking and sinful living. They become frustrated because in all of their trying, they either feel the same, or feel worse. When we return to the old covenant for deliverance, we depend on our earthly, sinful nature—our natural minds, apart from Christ. Apostle Paul describes the sinful nature in Romans 7:17-20. He says,

> As it is, it is no longer I myself who do it, but it is sin living in me. I know that nothing good lives in me, that is, in my sinful nature. For I have the desire to do what is good, but I cannot carry it out. For what I do is not the good I want to do; no, the evil I do not want to do—this I keep on doing. Now if I do what I do not want to do, it is no longer I who does it, but it is sin living in me that does it.
>
> Romans 7:17-20

Consistent with Paul's message, sinful habits seek to control our lives. Actually, because our minds are the property of sin in these instances, our minds work to gratify the sinful nature. And because our minds and the natures of sin are unified, sinful behaviors gratify our minds. This is a vicious cycle. Thus, sinful natures, which are our habits, rule our minds. Although sin is powerless, we grant it power when we attempt to deliver ourselves using human effort alone. Sin becomes victorious, because we provide it the power to torture our thinking.

Sin is powerless only when we live through Christ and His finished work at the cross, and when we understand the effect of grace. Living through Christ's finished work actually allows us to understand the purpose of grace. It allows us to abide in Him. When we abide in Christ, our minds create godly habits.

We are able to defeat sinful habits because godly habits and sinful habits cannot both exist in the same mind. They are incompatible habits. This means if one is present, then the other cannot exist. You may ask how this is possible. Well, if sinful habits exist in our minds, the Spirit will deal with us concerning these habits through conviction. If we do not respond to the Spirit's conviction, the sinful habit will remain in our minds; it may even lie dormant. If we respond to conviction by creating godly habits that are incompatible with sinful habits, the sinful habits will eventually cease.

ARE DRINKING AND SMOKING HABITS INSPIRED BY SATAN?

Habits that destroy our bodies are just as difficult to reverse as behaviors that have been regarded as sinful. This is because Satan, the father of deception and sin, has inspired both, sinful behaviors and behaviors that destroy the body. I've heard some say that drug habits, including cigarette and alcohol addiction, are not influenced by the deception of Satan and that people tend to engage in these activities on their own. This idea cannot be true considering God did not create us with a mind that will destroy us. Think about this for a moment before you disagree or agree with the statement. God did not create our minds to desire behaviors and activities that will destroy our bodies. Rather, the forces of Satan motivate us to engage in behaviors that gratify our minds, but eventually destroy our bodies.

If you were to create a valuable and sophisticated computer, would you create it with a built-in device that would blow the computer up the moment you turn it on? Of course not! Likewise, God did not create our minds to work, incessantly, to destroy our bodies. I'm not suggesting that computers are equivalent in design to the human mind, but my analogy reveals the foolishness of believing that we develop these habits on our own. Satan motivates habits that destroy the body of Christ. These include all habits that eventually destroy the body, including gluttonous eating habits. When we create habits that damage our bodies, we assist Satan with destroying the temple of God.

CHAPTER SUMMARY

Sanctification is a critical process of spiritual development and comprises at least two processes. The first process of sanctification is being removed from darkness to the presence of God upon accepting Christ as your Lord and Savior. The second process is allowing God to sanctify your mind by reading His Word and meditating and applying biblical principles.

Often, unbelievers dedicate their lives to God and are surprised that their behaviors do not change the moment of their acceptance. They may feel good emotionally about their dedication to God, but the next hour may reveal that their behaviors have not changed. The reason is they have experienced the first component of sanctification, in that God has taken them from darkness to light, but they must use mental abilities to allow God to sanctify their minds. They must read and meditate on the principles of God, and believe the Word will change their lives. This is a process of faith. From activating faith and applying biblical principles to their lives, they notice changes in their desires and in their behaviors. This is the second process of sanctification. Spiritual development will be hindered if we do not use our minds and mental abilities to process and apply the Word of God.

REFLECTION AND DISCUSSION QUESTIONS:

- Jot down what you believe was most meaningful from this chapter—something that you will share with a friend or colleague.
- How is this chapter relevant to your experiences in life?
- What "aha" moments did you have while reading this chapter?
- Reflect on Minister Doe's story at the start of this chapter. What caused him to lose sight of his calling?
- According to the chapter, why is it impossible to sanctify our minds if we do not apply ourselves—that is, if we do not read, pray, meditate, and believe what God's Word says is true?
- What is one thing you will change or reflect on more after having read this chapter?

SCRIPTURE TO REFLECT ON:
ROMANS 10:9

If you confess with your mouth, 'Jesus is Lord,' and believe in your heart that God raised Him from the dead, you will be saved.

WHAT'S NEXT?

In the next chapter, I discuss why we must be aware of our environments in order to create Godly habits, develop spiritually, and achieve success.

CHAPTER TWO:
BEWARE OF YOUR ENVIRONMENT: CREATING GODLY HABITS

Beware lest anyone cheat you through philosophy and empty deceit, according to the tradition of men, according to the basic principles of the world, and not according to Christ. For in Him dwells all the fullness of the Godhead bodily; and you are complete in Him, who is the head of all principality and power.

Colossians 2:8-10, NKJV

As a young boy, I lived in the John Hay Homes Housing Projects, in Springfield, Illinois. During this time, my family and I lived in poverty and received food stamps and food vouchers from the government. While living in the projects, my friends, siblings, and cousins would play tag and play at the park. While walking to the park, I recall seeing many signs on doors and gates that read, "Beware of dogs!" I have always been afraid of dogs so when I saw these signs, I would quickly run to the other side of the street. I would run quickly, while thinking, "What if these dogs jump the fence and attack me?" While running, my heart beat uncontrollably and I remained in a state of panic until I reached an area that I believed was safe. I would also look around for something to jump on should a dog escape the fence to attack me.

Like the projects I lived in, many communities post *beware* or *caution* signs on their doors or fences. These signs indicate warning: If someone enters a space without heeding these warning signs, they will place themselves at risk for danger. Therefore, warning signs provide anticipation. They forewarn.

Understanding the importance of warning signs is critical to developing spiritually and creating godly habits. We usually create sinful habits, because we do not construct warning signs in our minds. We allow our minds to enter places and associate with people who negatively affect our spirits.

To protect our spirits from the negativity that surrounds our environments, we must create warning signs that forewarn us of possible harm to our spiritual development. These warning signs should resemble something like the following:

- "Be cautious of Brother John or Sister Jones!"
- "Beware of that crowd of people!"
- "Beware of that movie!"
- "Beware of secular music that depresses your spirit!"
- "Beware of favoritism!"
- "Beware of that drink!"
- "Beware of that smoke!"
- "Be cautious of. . ."

Similar to how I was as a kid, we must be aware of our environments. We are often drained spiritually, because the things in our environments attack our spirits continuously. Our environments include anything we enter— our house, job, community, shopping center, church, and so on.

THE EFFECT OUR ENVIRONMENTS HAVE ON OUR MINDS

I have discussed how our subconscious minds are responsible for maintaining habits. Now I'll explain how our subconscious minds either develop us or destroy us mentally and spiritually.

Our subconscious minds pick up background information within our environments, information to which we pay little attention. We cannot control or monitor the information that enters our minds subconsciously. Once the information enters our minds, our spirits connect with it. For instance, if you have music playing in the background while reading this book, you may be consciously ignoring the music, but you may find yourself periodically humming, rocking, or tapping your finger to the music without your conscious awareness.

To use another example, you may be reading this book with music playing in the background, but once the music stops playing, and you take a break from this book, you may notice yourself subconsciously singing the lyrics or humming the beat that once played in the background. You may demonstrate these behaviors although the music has ended, and to your knowledge, you were attending to this book 100% while ignoring background information. Our mind's ability to gather and store information without our awareness is one reason why people behave in certain ways but have difficulty remembering where they had learned the particular behavior.

We have a tendency to replay what we perceive subconsciously, because information within our environments enters our minds without our awareness and incorporates itself within our spirits. This is problematic, because the spirit of sin dwells within our environments and presents its ugly face at our jobs, within our communities, within the school systems, and within churches, among other places. Although it is not a person per se, sin affects our minds, and works through us to provoke and antagonize each other.

The spirit of sin works through us to attempt to enter the minds of others, through their responses to our behaviors. This is why the Bible says, "In your anger, do not sin" (Ephesians 4:26). The spirit of sin inspires many things that gratify our flesh, including gaining revenge. Because we engage in these sinful behaviors for a prolonged period, they become habits.

Although sin feels good to our flesh, it eventually leads to destruction. We enter the space of sin, because we often refuse to heed the Bible's recommendations. We should realize that the Bible not only presents warning signs for earthly living, but also guides us in creating godly habits.

THE SOURCES BY WHICH SIN AFFECTS OUR MIND

Television is a telecommunication medium that advertises sinful behaviors better than most other media. Not only does television cater to visual learners by displaying pictures and visuals, but also to auditory learners. Television provides auditory learners with language and music that inhibit spiritual development. When we turn the television on, movies represent and glorify sinful behaviors such as fornication, stealing, lying, deception, wickedness, and adultery.

Nowadays, movies portray Jesus as an antichrist and encourage blasphemy of the Holy Spirit. These movies affect our minds without our knowing. We become a part of the sinful acts movies portray when we watch and interpret these behaviors. Although we do not experience the behaviors physically, we experience them mentally and spiritually. From watching certain movies, our minds generate desires. And as mentioned, we create habits from desiring sensation and believing that a need must be fulfilled.

Some behaviors we observe have a more detrimental effect on our minds and spirits than other behaviors. Generally, observing behaviors and activities we've been delivered from have the greatest effect on us. This explains why after we watch certain movies, we desire certain things, such as smoking, drinking, sexual promiscuity, cheating, and other behaviors from which Christ once delivered us.

Perceiving information subconsciously has both negative and positive consequences on our moods. For example, if we play gospel music or inspirational music while driving to work, the praise and worship music will fill our spirits subconsciously, or without our conscious awareness. Our spirits will be filled subconsciously although we may be preoccupied with driving and thinking about the many tasks we have to accomplish for the day; our spirits will be affected positively from the gospel music even though we aren't paying attention to it. Because background information affects our subconscious minds, we must be aware of our environments and create warning signs that will foretell possible danger to our development. Mental warning signs should encourage us to avoid behaviors to which we are most vulnerable, behaviors from which God has delivered us.

DESIRING HOLINESS

Now that you've learned the process by which we create habits, and now that you are familiar with the subconscious mind, let's consider behaviors that will lead to godly habits. In the following paragraphs, you'll come across eight steps that will make this possible. Remember, initially, creating habits starts with the conscious mind, which is our awareness. We become aware of environmental information and respond to it with repetition. The information that we must respond to with repetition, if we are to create godly habits, is the *Word* (see John 1:1-17 for a discussion of this Word).

Because we create habits from our desires, we must come to the decision that we desire God to sanctify our minds. We must also come to the decision that we desire to seek Christ, through His Word, to understand this process. Many people desire holiness. I've heard many sermons that focus on living holy. I've also heard Christian artists speak on the need for holiness in our generation. We should realize that sanctification leads to holiness as opposed to the reverse direction.

The Bible says we are to be holy because God is holy, but it is impossible to live holy without first allowing God to sanctify our minds. We experience sanctification when we live through Christ. We must allow God's Word to sanctify our minds because sinful habits dwell there, habits that conflict with holiness. It's impossible to live a holy life if we maintain sinful habits. From consciously separating ourselves from sinful activities and using our minds for sacred purposes, we'll come closer to the habits of God. I Thessalonians 4:3-8 makes this point clear:

> *It is God's will that you should be sanctified: that you should avoid sexual immorality; that each of you should learn to control his own body in a way that is holy and honorable, not in passionate lust like the heathen, who do not know God; and that in this matter no one should wrong his brother or take advantage of him. The Lord will punish men for all such sins, as we have already told you and warned you. For God did not call us to be impure, but to live a holy life. Therefore, he who rejects this instruction does not reject man but God, who gives you His Holy Spirit.*

I Thessalonians 4:3-8 speaks clearly of warning signs.

EIGHT BEHAVIORS TO CREATING GODLY HABITS

Eight simple steps can begin to establish godly habits as a foundation for your life.

1. **Pray in the morning.** Upon waking up in the morning, set aside a few minutes for prayer. Thank God for waking you and starting you on your way. Ask God to guide your walk and talk throughout the day. Finally, add your own quick personal prayer that you wish to share with God.

2. **Read.** Following your prayer, read an inspirational verse in the Bible, particularly from the book of Psalm or Proverbs. These Scriptures teach us how to behave as earthly beings. For example,

    -   Psalm 1:1 says, "Blessed is the man who does not walk in the counsel of the wicked or stand in the way of sinners or sit in the seat of mockers."
    -   Proverbs 1:5–6 says, "[L]et the wise listen and add to their learning, and let the discerning get guidance—for understanding proverbs and parables, the sayings and riddles of the wise."
    -   Proverbs chapter 1, verse 7, says, "The fear of God is the beginning of knowledge."

3. **Meditate.** Meditate on God periodically throughout the day, along with the Scripture you read that morning. Hymning a meaningful inspirational song to yourself will be helpful.

4. **Read again.** After your day is complete, read a chapter or two in the Bible before bed. Your nightly readings may be from books in the Bible not limited to Psalms or Proverbs.

5. **Pray nightly.** In your nightly prayer, thank God for walking with you throughout the day. Praise Him in advance for the mental strength you will receive the following day, and include your personal prayer.

6. **Reflect.** As you lie down to go to sleep, think about the outcome of your day and how you handled crises and disagreements. Did you let godly love influence your behaviors? If you notice that your actions were ungodly, think of strategies that may

potentially improve your behavior if you encounter the same problem in the future. Reflecting on the behaviors you displayed throughout the day and examining your feelings toward those behaviors won't be time-consuming. You'll be relaxed in bed, probably with your eyes closed, with your head propped on a pillow. It might make you go to sleep more quickly! Your focus should be on comparing the behaviors you displayed throughout the day to the Scriptures you read from the books of Psalms and Proverbs.

7. **Listen to the right music.** Limit your music to spiritual, inspirational music. Usually, Christian music incorporates Scripture. When you listen to godly music, you stimulate your subconscious mind with praise and worship, as opposed to music that condones sinful activities. Often, our attitudes during the day are the consequence of what we had heard prior to starting our day.

8. **Join a Christian Church**. It's imperative that you become a member of a Christian church. Becoming a member will give you access to an array of resources, including meeting people who are believers and learning the Bible from a pastor or priest. You'll also be able to ask questions and share personal concerns with members who are very familiar with God's Word.

If you engage in these eight steps with repetition, they'll eventually become habits. When you wake up in the morning, you'll find yourself getting off your knees from praying. You'll find yourself closing your Bible—after you've read your verse—and placing it back on the shelf. You'll also notice an increase in the amount of time you put into reading and praying.

Many people live their lives unaware of their behaviors toward others, because they act and react automatically and habitually. Since we often act without thinking, reflection (step six) is not procedural, but killing with our tongues is an ongoing practice. We fail to realize what may appear inoffensive to one person may bring catastrophe to another.

Step six, reflection, will allow us to become conscious of the way in which we treat others.

> *We all stumble in many ways. If anyone is never at fault in what he says, he is a perfect man, able to keep his whole body in check. When we put bits into the mouths of horses to make them obey us, we can turn the whole animal. Or take ships as an example. Although they are so large and are driven by strong winds, they are steered by a very small rudder wherever the pilot wants it to go. Likewise the tongue is a small part of the body, but it makes great boasts. Consider what a great forest is set on fire by a small spark. The tongue also is a fire, a world of evil among the parts of the body. It corrupts the whole person, sets the whole course of his life on fire, and is itself set on fire by hell.*

> James 3:2–6

THE ABILITY TO PRAISE GOD WITHOUT OUR CONSCIOUS AWARENESS

Rehearsing these eight behavioral steps will allow your mind to make spiritual procedures automatic, but only if you practice them until they become habitual. It is important that we are aware of our behaviors that have become habits. This awareness is imperative because the behaviors that we make habits are the behaviors most meaningful to our lives. Thus, they are the behaviors that identify our character, no matter how we portray or define our personality.

Creating godly habits spiritualizes our subconscious minds. Many people are saved by grace but questions remain:

- If believers are saved, why do they display ungodly behaviors so frequently?

- Why are believers so quick tempered?
- Why do some lie constantly?
- Why do believers . . .

Emotions, which our minds govern, cause people to react automatically in ungodly ways. People who react in ungodly ways have engaged in ungodly behaviors over a prolonged period, and when they become upset, they display ungodly behaviors without thinking. They have created these habits! At some point, we all respond negatively to our emotions. But the key question is, when behavioral responses are automatic, what behavior is your subconscious mind going to reveal?

WALKING WITH A NEW AGENDA

Once you incorporate godly behaviors, you will be able to walk away from confrontations with ease. Instead of bickering with the person who has harmed you, you will notice your spirit removing you from the situation. Now, in terms of the eight spiritual behaviors I discussed previously, the bickering situation would be placed into your nightly prayer, step five. Then, instead of plotting vengeance or considering how you could belittle the individual worse the next time, you will visualize how ungodly the altercation was and think of resolutions during reflection, step six.

The ability to create habits is the only way we're able to develop spiritually. I've heard people say they try to stay *God conscious* to remain saved. Staying God conscious sounds good, but is often difficult, given personal circumstances. The reality is, if we create the *habits* of God, we won't have to remain God conscious. Our subconscious minds will automatically produce God conscious behaviors, without our awareness or approval! From your godly habits, you will find people commending you on how you handled crises with ease and love; people will make comments on your ability to maintain joy in the midst of chaos; people will desire to imitate your behaviors, and in the process, will encounter Christ. Godly habits, in the above examples, actually reflect Christ ruling your mind. Your behaviors toward others reflect the fruit of His love.

From now on, attempt to notice your subconscious behaviors. Attempt to identify your actions when you display them automatically and work to correct them if they are ungodly. This is the essence of discipleship. Creating the habits of God is a process that consists of reading God's Word, praying, and separating yourself from people and events that encourage sinful activities. Remember, the key to creating godly habits is being aware of your environment, abiding in the Word of God, and creating mental warning signs that will allow you to foresee a potential attack on your spirit.

CHAPTER SUMMARY

In many communities, people have *beware* or *caution* signs on their doors or fences. These signs indicate warning: If someone enters space without heeding these warning signs, they will place themselves at risk for danger. Therefore, warning signs provide anticipation. They forewarn.

Spiritual development requires that we create warning and cautionary signs in our minds that forewarn us of a possible attack. Often, we place ourselves in the presence of people who are extremely negative, or enter spaces that encourage us to engage in behaviors from which God has delivered us. One reason why we must not surround ourselves with people who will disrupt the flow of God or enter spaces that might hinder our development is because our subconscious minds might pick up behaviors that will cause our development to regress to our old, sinful lifestyles. Developing spiritually requires that we seek God for supernatural knowledge about how to manage our behaviors and wisdom to discern when we should avoid places and people within our immediate environments.

REFLECTION AND DISCUSSION QUESTIONS:

- Jot down what you believe was most meaningful from this chapter—something that you will share with a friend or colleague.

- How is this chapter relevant to your experiences in life?

- What "aha" moments did you have while reading this chapter?

- Reflect on my story with living in housing projects and how I saw "beware of dogs" and "caution" signs within my neighborhood. Do you think it is important for us to create "mental signs" that forewarn us of a potential attack on our minds and spirits?

- What mental signs have you created to prevent an attack on your mind?

- Why is our subconscious mind responsible for maintaining habits?

- What will you do to create the habits of God?

- What is one thing you will change or reflect on more after having read this chapter?

SCRIPTURE TO REFLECT ON:
PROVERBS 1:5–6

[L]et the wise listen and add to their learning, and let the discerning get guidance . . .

WHAT'S NEXT?

In the next chapter, I will discuss the process of activating faith, which is your key to experiencing success in every area of your life!

CHAPTER THREE:
ACTIVATING FAITH: NECESSARY, SUFFICIENT, AND POWERFUL

You see, at just the right time, when we were still powerless,

Christ died for the ungodly. Very rarely will anyone die for a

righteous man, though for a good man someone might possibly

dare to die. But God demonstrates His own love for us in this:

While we were still sinners, Christ died for us.

Romans 5:6-8

On August 2, 2006, my wife gave birth to my son, Dwayne D. Williams II. It was a life- changing experience. I remember bringing him home from the hospital where he slept on my chest all night. Prior to Dwayne's birth, I had been submitting applications to school psychology programs in Illinois, praying that I would get accepted into a program to become a school psychologist. By the time Dwayne was born, I had been rejected from every school psychology program in Illinois. My rejection affected me tremendously. I experienced days of depression and doubt. Interestingly, I refused to give up on my dream of becoming a school psychologist and began applying to schools in other states.

Although I applied, I never intended to attend a program in a different state considering I had a son and wife to take care of. I had a bachelor's degree in psychology at this time and worked at a local behavioral hospital where I made about 15.00 dollars an hour. I recall spending countless hours at the library emailing school psychology directors in various states and leaving messages about how badly I wanted to become a school psychologist.

One day, to my surprise, one of the school psychology professors returned my call, a professor at Marshall University. During our conversation, I shared my story with him and shared that I was rejected from every school psychology program in Illinois because of my GRE scores. The professor explained that the staff at Marshall would give me a shot and that the faculty would save me a spot within the cohort, based on my personal essay and psychology GPA from undergraduate school. I was elated with the news. I would have an opportunity to become a school psychologist!

When I met with my wife in the evening, after speaking with the professor, my wife and I decided to pray about the opportunity. The decision was difficult, because our son Dwayne was literally a couple weeks old, we did not have jobs in Charleston, West Virginia—where the graduate program is located—and we did not have a lot of money saved.

Applying Faith

One day, as my wife and I prayed, I felt in my spirit that it was in God's will that I pursue the program in that He had opened a door for me that I should walk through. I spoke with my wife and she explained that she too felt that the Lord provided multiple signs for us to walk in faith, so that is what we did.

During the second week of my son's birth, my wife, family, and I packed up our belongings, wrapped up our two-week old son, and headed to West Virginia! We were walking in complete faith. We embarked on this venture with a newborn baby, we had no jobs in West Virginia, and had no idea what the apartment that we would live in looked like. My mother-in-law, who lived two hours away from the graduate program, looked around the area for an apartment for us. She found an apartment and secured our move-in date. We left our place of security, stepped out in faith, and believed God would provide for us. All I had was a few thousand dollars saved from working at the behavioral hospital, but I believed God!

THE STOREHOUSE

When we arrived to Charleston, West Virginia, we unloaded our furniture, then I rushed over to the graduate campus to introduce myself to the professor who accepted me into the program. "Hello, my name is Dwayne Williams. I just made it into town and I wanted to stop by to introduce myself and to say thank you for giving me an opportunity to pursue my dream!" As I walked in to introduce myself to the professor, the fax machine behind him was printing a document. Before he responded, he rolled in his chair over to the fax machine, while sitting in his chair, grabbed the fax, and handed me the document. "It's a pleasure to meet you, Dwayne! You will do just fine in our program. Here, take this document; it just started printing as you walked into the office. It looks like there is a professor at the undergraduate campus who is looking for a research assistant. If you are interested in this position, feel free to apply. I believe the position pays for college tuition and also provides a stipend."

When the professor handed me the document, tears began to fill my eyes. God had answered my prayers! My main concern regarding leaving my hometown was that I did not have a job to provide for my family, but I knew in my heart that God had opened a door for me to attend the program and that He wanted me to walk through that door and trust Him. I applied for the job and was hired on the spot. Not only did God bless me with a job upon arriving to Charleston, West Virginia, but He also made it possible for the school to pay my tuition!

From walking through this door, I eventually graduated with two master's degrees and landed a job as a school psychologist immediately after graduating. In addition to landing a job, I eventually wrote several books on the topic of increasing performance among African American students—a topic that I studied while at Marshall University—and I established my own organization where I travel the country in which I train educators on my research. In fact, I have trained the very professors who rejected me from their programs!

Is there something that God is pushing you to do but you are afraid to step out in faith? If I had not stepped out in faith, I would have never accessed the resources that He stored away for me. Earlier I explained that all that we desire that is in the will of God has already been set aside for our pleasure. In order for me to receive what God had for me, my career, I had to operate in faith and believe that He would supply my needs. What if I had not activated faith and believed that He would not provide for me while in Charleston?

ACTIVE FAITH

Most believers understand that God's Word requires us to activate and live by faith, but why does God place great emphasis on faith? If you ask believers why we must live by faith, most would probably quote Hebrews 11:6, which says, "[W]ithout faith, it is impossible to please God, because anyone who comes to [H]im must believe that [H]e exists and that [H]e rewards those who earnestly seek Him."

But why is it *impossible* to please God without activating faith in Him? Why are we required to activate faith to experience God's power? The answer is active faith is a *divine attribute.* That is, it characterizes the behaviors of God. It may sound a bit unusual to say that active faith characterizes God's behaviors. In order to understand ,let's define the term *active faith* and apply it to His actions.

The term *active* describes activity that is marked by energy or exertion. It should go without saying that, to be active, one must engage in movement of some kind and work to initiate or complete an objective.

On the other hand, "Now Faith is the substance of things hoped for, the evidence of things not seen" (Hebrews 11:1, NKJV). Faith is the act of believing in what is hoped for, although one's desire or hope may not be present or visible. To the human mind, active faith is unusual because the principle of faith requires us to start at success and work backward, as if we have already attained our desired goal. It requires us to not only believe but also to know in our hearts that whatever we ask or speak in the spiritual realm will manifest in the natural realm. This means we are required to see success, although we may perceive chaos, emptiness, or darkness in our daily lives.

What does it mean to start at success? This concept means that, prior to embarking on some goal, we must see success in our minds, no matter what we see with our eyes. In other words, we must envision success no matter how difficult our problems may appear. This idea characterizes God's behaviors. Genesis 1:2 tells us that, prior to God's creation of earth, it was "formless and empty, darkness was over the surface of the deep." Directly following this verse, the Scripture says ". . .and the Spirit of God was hovering over the waters."

The fact that God was hovering over the waters, in the midst of a formless, empty and dark earth, suggests that God did not let what was *visible* dissuade His vision. Rather, He placed Himself in the midst of chaos and created order and life. Genesis could have simply stated that God created the earth, period. I believe the Scripture described the earth's condition—formless, empty and dark space—to show the power of God, that He can improve any situation and condition.

Actually, the Scripture does two things: The first is it shows the relationship between God's behaviors and how He requires us to behave in the spiritual realm, which the Bible describes as active faith; the second is testimonial—it shows us that, no matter what our condition looks like, God can rework and reroute our situation. It shows us that God can create success from our emptiness, chaos, and mess!

God's creation of earth shows us that success starts first at the spiritual realm, through believing God will move on our behalf. When we allow God to use our minds—mental action—our success materializes at the earthly realm. Our actions materialize what is spiritual.

Merriam Webster's Collegiate Dictionary defines the term *materialize* like this: "To cause to appear in bodily form." When we materialize what is spiritual, we not only see success, but we also, ourselves, become successful. We become the object of success that we had initially envisioned. Now get this: Because of our success in Christ, when we pursue a goal, we know that we can ask anything in His name and God will not only hear us, but also provide for us according to His will.

LET THERE BE LIGHT

Upon the creation of the Universe, God envisioned a plan and pro-actively spoke existence upon His plan: "And God said, 'Let there be light,' and there was light. God saw that the light was good and He separated light from darkness" (Genesis 1:3-4).

Genesis 1:3-4 sheds more light on God's behaviors. Prior to creating light, God not only *hoped* for its presence but He also hoped to distinguish it from darkness. That which was hoped for was the *substance* of God's desire. In other words, God believed His Word would fulfill a desired outcome, although the outcome was not yet visible. God's calling light into existence and His separating light from darkness caused what He hoped to become reality. He materialized what was spiritual.

Understanding that active faith is a divine attribute is the first step in attaining what you desire. You might say, "How is it that God's behaviors characterize faith when, after all, God is all-knowing?"

I'm glad you asked!

First, realize that I am saying that His behaviors characterize active faith; this means His behaviors demonstrate what active faith looks like.

Think about it like this. Because God is all-knowing, He is unable to doubt His abilities. He knows, without a shadow of doubt, that He will accomplish what He desires. He knows that when He speaks, His Word creates; it materializes, for Isaiah 55:10-11 (NKJV):

> *For as the rain comes down, and the snow from heaven, and*
>
> *do not return there, but water the earth, and make it bring*
>
> *forth and bud, that it may give seed to the sower and bread to*
>
> *the eater, so shall My word be that goes forth from My mouth;*
>
> *it shall not return to Me void, but it shall accomplish what I*
>
> *please, and it shall prosper in the thing for which I sent it.*

Stated simply, God believes in Himself. He believes His Word and provides a perfect example of what active faith looks like. God actually uses His abilities—creating life out of emptiness and darkness—as models for us. Therefore, if you want to know what faith looks like, refer to the behaviors of God; read His Word.

Someone else may say that because God is all-knowing and because He can see what is not present, that His behaviors do not characterize active faith. They may support their reasoning by saying that faith is believing what is unseen, and since God sees both what is seen and unseen, His behaviors are not characteristic of faith. Well, get this: As His children, we are also all-knowing in terms of what we can and can't do; we are able to see what is seen and unseen when it comes to declaring our success in Christ. I'll show you how.

Prior to setting goals, you usually know what you want to do. You can see your failures and potential embarrassments should you fail to meet your goal or expectation. But you can also see your success if you look for it; that is, if you believe, you will experience success. We usually see our performance in our minds prior to acting. We usually see the result of our goals. The result is usually consistent with our belief prior to starting the goal. The reality is we can control our thoughts and control what we see. If we believe and meditate on failing, we will fail. If we believe and meditate on success, we will succeed. In my story at the start of this chapter, I saw my success. My wife and I envisioned God showing us favor, which is exactly what He did.

You may say, "I can see myself becoming successful." You may contemplate your success all day. The problem is you may fantasize about your success, which means your success is mental only; it doesn't materialize but remains in your mind. The difference between our knowing and God's knowing, then, is this: He knows, believes, and acts; we usually know, fantasize, and refuse to act.

We usually see what we can't do. Because we focus on what is physical and visible, we usually don't see success, let alone feel successful. We limit the things that we believe we can do. Now get this: God attempts to get us to think like Him, not only to believe in Him and His abilities, but also that we can do all things through Him. He says that through Him, all things are possible. In fact, God's Word says, "No eye has seen, no ear has heard, no mind has conceived what God has prepared for those who love Him" (I Corinthians 2:9). Prior to acting, God's Spirit sees what we hope and goes beyond our thoughts to provide for us.

The fact that God's behaviors are characteristic of faith means that faith is not some meaningless thought. Rather, faith is a divine attribute that we activate for a particular cause; it is an attribute that we must activate to access all that God has in store for us. In the above example,

God showed how His activity resulted in dividing light and darkness into morning and night (Genesis 1:3-5). Morning and night represent the *effect* of an initial desire, a desire for which God once hoped. A world consisting of morning and night was the final product of God's actions.

God's behaviors show there is a cause-effect relationship between activity and faith at the earthly level. God believed in some outcome and worked toward the intangible. His behaviors show that faith is the belief in the intangible. *Activity* is the means to the tangible.

To use another example, before God transformed Himself into flesh, His *hope* was to redeem humankind of their sins. God's hope characterized what we know as "the substance of faith." Hope and belief laid the foundation of His plan. Redemption was the cause. Transforming His godly making into flesh, dying on the cross, and rising for our justification were the activities that materialized His hope. Salvation and grace were the effects, the consequences of His behaviors. Salvation and grace were the outcomes of what He hoped to accomplish. God's belief in the intangible and His active works brought fruition to His desires.

THE SUBSTANCE OF FAITH

Notice that the *substance* of faith is a key attribute of faith. In the earthly realm, substance is the internal, immaterial nature of human beings that is connected to wants and needs. As an example, have you noticed that people tend to rely on faith more frequently and more consistently when crises arise? This is because the substance of our faith is attached to *things* that are outside of our control. I believe God designed this connection this way to allow us to understand that some needs require supernatural blessings. And supernatural blessings require supernatural faith, such as believing in an unseen God and understanding that He will reward those who earnestly seek Him (Hebrews 11:6).

Take a moment to reflect on what you were doing on September 11, 2001, also known as 9/11. On this day, I was in a psychology class, at a community college. After my instructor ended his lecture, I walked out of the classroom to a vast amount of students gathered around a flat screen television in the cafeteria. Many of the students were crying hysterically, while others looked as if they had lost all hope. Most all students appeared frightened by what they saw.

As I began to watch the news on the screen, I had noticed people of all races and backgrounds hugging each other, crying, and praying. Our country had experienced a crisis. Collectively, the American people relied on God, probably more than any other time in their lives, during this troubling moment in history. Their collective prayers showed that the substance of their faith was connected to some need they themselves could not fulfill.

Many people read the Bible repeatedly and memorize Scriptures regarding faith. It's important to realize, however, that faithfully *believing* and *understanding* faith are two separate processes. You can read and understand information regarding faith, but if you are not practicing faith-based principles, you're only quoting Scriptures, and are therefore doing nothing more than simply biblically commentating—speaking and acting in the absence of power. Faith requires action on our part. Our action is what opens doors to our storehouse. When we *act* in belief, although our desires may appear impossible to obtain with human abilities alone, we show God that we have confidence in His Word. We show God that we believe His promises.

> *What good is it, my brothers, if a man claims to have faith but has no deeds? Can such faith save him?*

> James 2:14

Is your faith supported by deeds? You now have an understanding of active faith that is required to access all that God has for you. You also understand that active faith will bring your purpose to fruition. At this moment, look inward and think about your faith. Have you placed your faith in God? If so, are you allowing Him to use your mind and abilities to materialize success in your life and the lives of others? These questions may show you why you have or have not obtained your desired goals. If you find difficulty reaching goals or experiencing success, take a closer look at your faith. Understand that active faith is what inspires God to meet your wants and needs; it is a requisite to access all that is within your storehouse.

WHY FAITH?

Romans chapter 1, verse 17, says that the righteous will live by faith. It is through faith that we secure our knowledge about God. This statement is the most essential aspect of our walk with God and spiritual development. God has revealed Himself throughout our history, but without faith, we are unable to interpret His works. Therefore, faith is the lens by which we understand God and His behaviors.

When faith is inactive, we do not see God, although He often stands directly in front of us. People who live by faith usually say, "God got me out of that situation!" Their statement shows that they see God in their history; they see God as their deliverer. People whose faith is inactive usually say, "I don't see why you give God credit for everything. I just don't see it!" Their blindness should not surprise us. When these people experience some level of success that was unimaginable for them, they say, "Wow, I can't believe I [fill in the blank with whatever success]." They do not attribute their success to the hand of God; they usually attribute their success to their own abilities, favor from man, relationships, connections, or some other factor.

The Bible says that God's divine qualities have been clearly shown to us (Romans 1:19-20, NKJV). But it is through faith that we connect God to the qualities of which the Bible speaks. Thus, we *see* Christ in our lives through faith. Let's take for example the Israelites and their experiences in Egypt to illustrate how we see God. The Israelites knew God. God was a part of their history. Although their vision was not always clear, their faith allowed them to *see* God in the midst of their struggles. Exodus 14:30 (NKJV) says,

> So the Lord saved Israel that day out of the hand of the
> Egyptians, and Israel saw the Egyptians dead on the seashore.
> Thus Israel saw the great work which the Lord had done in

Egypt; so the people feared the Lord, and believed the Lord and

His servant Moses.

Because of their strengthened faith, they knew, without any doubt, that *God* delivered them from the hands of Pharaoh. Exodus 15:1-3 (NKJV) tells us,

Then Moses and the children of Israel sang this song to the Lord, and spoke, saying: I will sing to the Lord, for He has triumphed gloriously! The horse and its rider He has thrown into the sea! The Lord is my strength and song, and He has become my salvation; He is my God, and I will praise Him.

If the Israelites refused to identify God as their deliverer, they would have attributed their deliverance to something or someone other than Him. Their faith, at that point in their life, allowed them to interpret God's behaviors and understand His presence in their history.

WITHOUT FAITH, WE DO NOT SEE GOD

Although God delivered the Israelites from Egyptian slavery, they began to lose faith in Him. They removed the lens they used to interpret God's hand in their history. Consequently, they did not see God. Instead of worshipping their Lord, the Israelites requested that Aaron make an idol god for their worship. In response to their request, Aaron said, "Break off the golden earrings which are in the ears of your wives, your sons, and your daughters, and bring them to me" (Exodus 32:2, NKJV). Aaron collected the gold from the Israelites and molded a golden calf.

After Aaron molded the golden calf, the Israelites proclaimed, "This is your god, O Israel that brought you out of the land of Egypt!" The Israelites worshipped this golden calf as their savior and offered burnt offerings and peace offerings before it. Essentially, the Israelites lost sight of God. Consequently, they worshipped the treasure God had blessed them with instead of worshipping God Himself! Exodus 32:1-6 is significant. It shows us that when we do not remain in faith, we lose sight of God. We no longer *see* Him in our history. Consequently, we glorify the things He created for us as opposed to glorifying Him.

Like the Israelites, prior to deactivating their faith, we must allow our faith to interpret God's work in our history. Since God's activity in our lives is based on pure belief, if we do not activate faith to present ourselves to Him, we'll never experience His actions. Understanding that God is an ambassador of faith and His actions bring about results, I'm endowed with a feeling of pure trust because I understand there is an ultimate faith that supersedes all doubt. I understand that we can look toward the hills for our help, and that our help comes from the Lord (Psalms 121:1-2).

For spiritual purposes, faith in Christ's work at the cross is required in order to *receive* forgiveness for your sins. Notice that faith is required for you to receive. I mentioned "receive" because God has already done all that He will ever do for you, and that includes forgiving you for your sins. Your job is to *confess* and then *receive* (believe) what He has done. You can't simply *wish* that God would forgive you from sinful behaviors and sinful thinking. This is an example of starting at success. When you confess and believe that God has forgiven you and will renew your mind, your starting point will be successful.

For natural purposes, active faith is the precursor to re-attaining all that the adversary has stolen from you. Allow me to reiterate this point. The phrase, "What the adversary has stolen from you" does not suggest materialistic possessions only, but also attributes that effect your mind.

This means if your joy has been stolen, active faith will re-establish joy; if your confidence has been stolen, active faith will build confidence; if your ability to love has been stolen, active faith will ignite love; and if your faith has been stolen, seeking the face of God to activate your faith will restore your belief. Remember, activating faith starts with believing that both you and God must fulfill a purpose.

This righteousness from God comes through faith in Jesus Christ
to all who believe. There is no difference, for all have sinned
and fall short of the glory of God, and are justified freely by

His grace through the redemption that came by Christ Jesus.
God presented Him as a sacrifice of atonement, through faith
in His blood.

Romans 3:22-25

I NEVER SEE THE POWER OF FAITH!

But you will receive power when the Holy Spirit comes on you.

Acts 1:8

Many people admit they never experience the power of which the Bible speaks. Their statement shows they believe that God's dying on the cross is powerless and apparently contradictory to them. If Christ has already redeemed and justified us by His actions on the cross, why are the minds of many still in bondage? The answer is clear: "Without faith it is impossible to please God, because anyone who comes to Him must believe that He exists and that He rewards those who earnestly seek Him" (Hebrews 11:6). Put another way, it is pointless to pray to God but refuse to believe in His eternal existence and divine power.

Hebrews 11:6 concisely explains why people rarely experience the power of faith. Many people do not experience the *glory* of God, His honor and His power, because they superficially believe in His existence. They have a difficult time believing that the Holy Spirit indwells them. Some people have a difficult time believing that the Holy Spirit lives in them, because they have not experienced spiritual gifts. Unfortunately, sometime in their spiritual development, these people were taught that the only evidence of the Spirit is demonstrating spiritual gifts, like speaking in unknown tongues, for example. Because these people have not spoken in unknown tongues, they believe the Holy Spirit does not indwell them, although they have confessed Christ into their lives and believe, without any doubt, that He has died for their sins.

They do not understand that their ability to do what they were unable to do prior to accepting Christ into their life is the manifestation of the Holy Spirit. They do not realize that the Holy Spirit is allowing them to forgive the person they were unable to forgive with human abilities alone; they don't realize that it is the Holy Spirit that is giving them power to remove themselves from sinful activities, activities they were unable to remove themselves from prior to accepting the Spirit into their lives.

These people fail to understand that the Holy Spirit allows them to speak about God to their friends with power and conviction, and that their ability to speak effectively in people's lives is not a reflection of some talent or skill they have created. Essentially, these people believe that the verse, "You will receive power when the Holy Spirit comes on you" refers strictly to speaking in tongues or some other spiritual gift. Consequently, they fail to perceive the power of God in their lives. They fail to see that their ability to do what they could not do prior to accepting Christ is also the manifestation of the power of the Holy Spirit. They fail to understand that the power of God is not limited to demonstrating spiritual gifts, but also it softens our hearts and allows us to love those we previously despised.

Others have not experienced the power of God, because they superficially believe in Christ's existence: That is, they believe what they had been told by others. This means these individuals believed in their storytellers, as opposed to acquiring a personal relationship with Christ and allowing Christ to manifest His glory to them personally.

INACTIVE FAITH

Many people have faith that has the potential to move God, but their faith is inactive. Their faith is present in mind and spirit, but these people do not demonstrate faith in their behaviors and actions; they believe in God's existence and power, but they do not actively involve themselves in obtaining desired goals. I repeat: *They do not actively involve themselves!*

These people tend to stack all of their problems at heaven's door and leave them there. And stacking their problems does not mean they lie prostrate before God, while stating their weaknesses. After all, lying prostrate before God to gain strength is taking action in their deliverance. Instead, they compile all of their problems and hand them over to God. They believe they can consciously create sinful habits and simply give them to Jesus when the going gets tough. Yes, we can give our problems to God, but His Word shows that we must pair faith with action. So the question is, are we actively seeking deliverance from the things that weigh us down spiritually? Or are we handicapping ourselves by *thinking*, "God will do it!" instead of *actively believing* He will do it?

The adversary tries to deceive us into believing that faith has to be abundant to please God. Consequently, many people find it difficult to activate their faith. Their thoughts are usually something like "I just don't have enough faith to move God!" According to Luke 17:5-6, the magnitude of faith is comparable to that of a mustard seed. When we realize that God has instilled a measure of faith within us all, activating our faith will be less difficult.

Jesus taught His apostles that, through faith, God is capable of doing the impossible:

> *The apostles said to the Lord, 'Increase our faith!' He replied,*
> *'If you have faith as small as a mustard seed, you can say to this*
> *Mulberry tree, Be uprooted and planted in the sea,' and it*
> *will obey you*

Luke 17:5-6).

RELEASING OURSELVES

Since Christ released us by dying on the cross, we must release ourselves by actively putting ourselves in positions that will allow God to reveal His glory. That is exactly what I did (see my story at the start of this chapter) and from my belief and action, I am pursuing my heart's desire.

My question to you is this: If you are fearful, how will you ever experience God's power, deliverance, and access your storehouse if you constantly avoid your fears? Likewise, how will you ever experience your deliverance from addiction(s) if you continue to depend on substances, as opposed to depending on God's promises? If you have difficulty believing in God, how will you ever allow Christ to reveal Himself to you unless you activate your faith?

Many believers act like infants when they approach God. When infants are hungry, they will cry until someone feeds them. They will cry until they are satisfied. Many believers demonstrate this same infantile behavior, but unfortunately, God will leave us crying if we do not actively step out in faith for the purpose of deliverance. Many believers are crying, in the form of depression and stress, because they have been waiting on God to perform a miracle for them. These individuals "wait" on God instead of believing in their deliverance and putting themselves in positions to witness God's power.

Positioning ourselves so God can reveal Himself is actually mental and spiritual activity. We must face our fears by putting ourselves in positions that we know only the power of God can get us out. We realize deliverance through these experiences. The next time an opportunity presents itself for you to face your fears, no matter what your mind tells you about your incompetence and inability, step out in faith and know that God will make provisions for you. And if you step out in faith and believe you have failed once again, realize that your breakthrough is on the way. This is faith.

Multiple failures create character if we persevere through our storms. Multiple failures show that we continued to persevere and believed in God's Word in the midst of unsuccessful experiences. Seeking the face of God to bring us through when we continue to fail is true faith! It's easy to trust God when we experience success directly following our moment of prayer. But the measure of faith is this: What happens when you pray to God and then fail immediately after praying, and continue to fail in that same area? Is your faith strengthened or shaken by these experiences?

DISBELIEF IS OPPOSITIONAL FAITH

Why are we so fearful of the things Christ has already defeated on this earth by dying on the cross, but we are fearless when it comes to opposing

God? When we boldly oppose God, we *believe* that we do not have to activate faith to access what God has stored away for us. We engage in what I call *oppositional faith* whenever we disbelieve. Oppositional faith is in stark contrast with the faith that characterizes God.

The idea of oppositional faith indicates that it is impossible to have complete doubt. Even during moments of disbelief, we believe in something that causes our disbelief. For example, if you doubt your ability to become successful in today's world, you actually believe you lack the skills and competence needed to produce success. If you doubt your ability to overcome addictions, you actually believe your addictions have taken authority and dominion over your life. And if you doubt God's existence, you actually believe there is a better explanation for the creation of life. Many people remain distant from God because their faith is oppositional. Likewise, many are unable to experience deliverance from addictive substances because of oppositional faith.

Oppositional faith is often domain specific. This means, one could have faith that God exists, but have oppositional faith in other areas. For example, one may believe in the existence of God and believe in Christ's resurrection, but in the domain of addictions, their faith may be oppositional. These individuals may believe the power of God cannot deliver them. We remain distant from God in areas where oppositional faith characterizes our belief.

If you are guilty of activating oppositional faith, which, again, is what disbelief actually is, allow God to restore the faith of Matthew 13:31-32. I'm pleased to assure you that the activation process is not time consuming if you are willing to activate minute faith.

Remember, faith does not have to be abundant to please God. If you are one who refused to learn of God, I have a few questions for you:
- Why not give God a try?
- Why not make a change in your stabilized belief?
- What will you lose by learning of God's true existence?

You have taken the first step by reading this book, but at this very moment, I challenge you to open your heart and allow God to manifest His glory to you. In the process of your seeking God, remember this important truth: "The righteous will live by faith" (Romans 1:17).

CHAPTER SUMMARY

God attempts to get us to think like Him. Throughout the Bible, He shows why active faith is a necessary, efficient, and powerful component to not only developing spiritually, but also to experiencing success in every area of your life. Why is active faith such an important component of spiritual development? The answer is, active faith is a divine attribute and characterizes God's behaviors.

God's behaviors show there is a cause-effect relationship between activity and faith at the earthly level. Active faith is a divine attribute that allows us to access all that God has stored away for us; it is the component of spiritual development that will allow you to experience success in every area of your life. In fact, it will bring heaven to earth!

REFLECTION AND DISCUSSION QUESTIONS:

- Jot down what you believe was most meaningful from this chapter—something that you will share with a friend or colleague.

- How is this chapter relevant to your experiences in life?

- What "aha" moments did you have while reading this chapter?

- Reflect on my story in which I believed God would provide for my family. I walked in faith and accessed my blessing the moment I arrived at the graduate campus. What has God been telling you to do that you have been afraid to pursue?

- What will you do to activate your faith?

- What is one thing you will change or reflect on more after having read this chapter?

SCRIPTURE TO REFLECT ON:
HEBREWS 11:6

[W]ithout faith, it is impossible to please God, because anyone who comes to [H]im must believe that [H]e exists and that [H]e rewards those who earnestly seek Him.

WHAT'S NEXT?

In the next chapter, I discuss the relationship between confidence and faith. I explain the confidence that we have in Jesus. Usually, we either discuss faith *or* confidence; rarely do we discuss faith and confidence as interrelated components to development. The next chapter sheds light on this concept!

CHAPTER FOUR:
The Relationship between
Confidence and Faith

This is the confidence we have in approaching God: that if we ask anything according to His will, He hears us. And if we know He hears us— whatever we ask—we know that we have what we asked of Him.

I John 5:14-15

As a success coach, I work with clients from various backgrounds, clients who desire to advance in their careers. The majority of my clients desire to advance by publishing books, speaking publically, and becoming consultants and coaches. From working with these individuals, I have found that the majority of them have faith that they could go from where they currently are in their careers, to where they want to be. Although they have faith, many of them lack an important attribute, which is confidence.

I Know that I Have the Skills to Write Books!

One day while meeting with one of my clients, he and I talked about his desire to write a book. This client is amazingly gifted and talented; he is tremendously skillful—a jack of many trades. I will call this client Bobby to avoid disclosing his real name. During our meeting, I asked, "Bobby, what have you been doing about your book? Any progress?" "Well, Dwayne," Bobby explained, "I have been doing a lot of thinking. I know that I have a story to tell and I know that once I get started, God will make a way and will assist me throughout the process. I help people solve problems daily and meet their goals, and so I have many success stories that will encourage others. Dwayne, with the Lord's help, I know that I could get it done. I am more than convinced!"

Bobby spoke passionately and positively about his ability to write a book. He stated that eventually he will publish and that he knows his book will open doors to speaking engagements, including doors that have been previously slammed in his face; he also talked about how speaking engagements would advance his career. He stated that, with the help of God, and with my direction as his coach, he could become a successful writer and consultant. While he rambled on and on about how much faith he had in the area of writing a book, I interrupted him. "Bobby, it is clear that you believe, with God's help, and with a little direction, that you could advance your career by publishing and speaking publically; you know that you have the skills and you explained that you are a decent writer. Why haven't you gotten started yet?"

From Bobby's response, we both identified the problem: "Dwayne, I think about writing all the time. The things that keep me from writing are my own thoughts. I often think, 'Who will want to read a book written by me? I feel that I will invest a lot of time writing and am afraid that no one will want to read a book that I write. Why would anyone want to read a book that I publish?"

When Bobby spoke, he emphasized "I" and "me"—why would anyone want to read a book that *I* write, a book written by *me*. The barrier that prevented Bobby's writing was not lack of faith, for his faith was larger than the size of a mustard seed, and it was evident. Bobby lacked confidence.

CONFIDENCE AND FAITH

Ask any believer what faith means and they'll tell you. Some will even explain the concept of hope that is inherent in faith-based messages. But one attribute that believers rarely discuss is confidence as it relates to faith. In the earthly realm, confidence is the attribute that moves us toward God, but in the spiritual realm, faith is the substance that moves God. Thus, confidence and faith are key attributes that allow us to experience God's glory. It's important to realize that God's Spirit leads us to Christ, not confidence or any other human attribute or ability; it is also God's power that allows our confidence in His Word. Does this mean that God's power is weak when people fail to show confidence in His Word? Absolutely not. It shows their disbelief in His power!

Understanding the relationship between confidence and faith is critical for spiritual development. As mentioned, God has given a measure of faith to us all. Our job is to activate such faith. Contrarily, we must learn confidence. Without confidence and faith, we lack hope and are full of doubt. Because we rarely discuss confidence within the same context of faith and hope, its mention may appear a bit unusual. Actually, lack of confidence in God's Word explains why people doubt God's existence; it is the main reason many struggle with activating their faith.

The process of activating faith deals fundamentally with confidence. Our minds must be persuaded in order to believe in anything. The earthly mind operates by logic as it pertains to cause-and-effect phenomena. The mind has to believe that a cause will produce an actual effect. Not only does the mind prefer logic, but the logic must also be reliable. This means the cause must consistently produce the same effect over time. For example, if you throw a ball against a wall, you expect the ball to bounce off the wall; you do not expect the ball to seep through the wall and disappear. You would expect the ball to bounce back each time you throw it against the wall. Faith does not operate by this type of logic. Because our minds are used to this consistent, cause-and-effect order, many people have difficulty establishing confidence to approach God, and this may be the number one reason they are unable to operate in faith and unable to access all that God has stored away for their pleasure.

THE PURPOSE OF FAITH

Faith does not always lead to consistent, back-to-back outcomes, as our minds might prefer. But producing consistent, back-to-back outcomes is not the purpose of faith. The purpose of faith is to develop us as spiritual beings. This means faith develops us even when we believe we do not hear from God on a daily basis. It develops us even when we feel God has abandoned us. In fact, when outcomes are not as consistent as our minds might prefer, faith in God is what allows our joy. Essentially, faith in Christ leads to spiritual development and the more our faith increases, the more growth in Christ we experience.

Although faith leads to the same outcome—spiritual development—the process by which we experience faith's effect on our lives varies by person. It varies according to the call God has on our lives. If part of my calling is to witness to those who have trouble learning confidence, faith will develop my ministry. This means the effect of faith as it pertains to confidence will be different for me than it will be for you. If my calling is to work with those who lack confidence, at some point, my experiences will have allowed me to know what lacking confidence feels like. The process of faith will allow this. And at some point, this process may be difficult for me to understand lest God reveals His purpose. This means that faith has a purpose and is governed by God's destined will. Faith leads us to our destination, which means your faith may have a different course of action than my faith, although we may have the same goal. This is why the earthly mind regards faith as unreliable. Although faith may lead us into different directions, based on our experiences, it leads to one truth, that it is impossible to please God without it (Hebrews 11:6).

UNDERSTANDING CONFIDENCE

We respond to what we see. It is not with our eyes that we see, but with our minds. Our eyes are the mechanisms used to view the external world. Our minds provide vision. Because the mind cannot see the faith that God provides, it rejects it. Therefore, we must lean toward confidence in the earthly realm to activate faith in the spiritual realm. Let's define confidence to better appreciate the latter statement.

Confidence is full trust or belief in the reliability of a person or thing. We usually gain confidence in a person or thing *after* we establish full trust in them. In other words, confidence is a mental phenomenon that we learn, which explains why we are unsure of people or things until trust is established. Based on this explanation, confidence is a term used to explain a phenomenon that the mind experiences. *Confidence* is actually the result of successful outcomes or perceptions that produced belief. In the opening story of this chapter, the barrier that interfered with Bobby's progress was confidence, which eventually affected his self-esteem and self-perceptions. He could not see himself as an established writer. He could not phantom the idea that people would want to read his thoughts, so he engaged in a continual cycle of procrastination.

CHEMICAL RESPONSES

The phenomenon that we call confidence is an effect of chemical responses that occur when the mind encounters experiences that once led to success. Because the mind is used to cause-and-effect phenomena, it believes that experiences similar to those that brought about success will also result in success.

These experiences extend to people and abilities. We have confidence in certain people and our abilities, because they once provided success for us in the past. We reflect on these successful experiences to establish goals. In the same manner, when we experience failure, our minds remember these moments. When similar situations, opportunities, or people come around that resemble failure, chemical responses produce within our minds, which causes us to doubt.

Many psychologists have identified confidence as a predictor of success, because it carries over from experiences. As such, people who have succeeded in the past expect to succeed in the future. When these individuals prepare, chemical responses that produce confidence overtake their minds. They prepare for their ventures and usually attain success. Those who expect to fail, fail to prepare adequately, and in most cases, chemicals that lead to doubt consume their minds. The fact that confidence is an indicator of success doesn't refer to earthly success only, but also to spiritual success.

HOW TO ACTIVATE FAITH IN CARNAL MINDS

Confidence in God must lead to the activation of faith, because, although nonbelievers have the ability to produce faith, they do not understand the purpose of faith, or the attributes of the Spirit. The reason is biblical: "But the natural man does not receive the things of the Spirit of God, for they are foolishness to him; nor can he know them, because they are spiritually discerned" (I Corinthians 2:14, NKJV). This verse teaches us that the natural mind will reject the things from God and will not apply godly principles to life, for these principles are too spiritual for the natural mind to comprehend.

Because the natural mind tends to trust those things that have led to success in the past, people of doubt must first have the confidence to approach God in order to experience the effect of faith. People who doubt must gain confidence to approach God so that He can activate their faith. They must have confidence that He will catch them when they fall. It's important that we realize confidence doesn't activate faith. Confidence pushes those who doubt in the direction of God. Once they are in God's presence, His glory will activate faith, based on their willingness to believe in His work.

> *Such confidence as this is ours through Christ before God.*
> *Not that we are competent in ourselves to claim anything for*
> *ourselves, but our competence comes from God.*

> II Corinthians 3:4-5

Because the natural mind focuses on what is seen, how do we push nonbelievers and people of oppositional faith in the direction of God? Because the natural mind responds best to what is visible, we must present Christ in an observable, physical form. We must allow what is spiritual to manifest into flesh. Believers must become that fleshly image. We must demonstrate Christ through our behaviors. We do this by allowing Him to use our physical beings to represent His Sprit. We allow God to use us by renewing our minds, sharing His Spirit, and digesting His Word.

A major problem with believers is many people who represent Christ act similarly to individuals who refuse to renew their minds. They are easily angered, lie continuously, deceive, condone violence, smoke, drink, and the list goes on. Consequently, those who find difficulty separating themselves from the world's pleasures also find difficulty gaining confidence in God. As such, when we attempt to push them toward Christ, they are not convinced that He can deliver them. Moreover, some nonbelievers refuse to activate faith in God, because they constantly observe believers demonstrating behaviors that do not typify godly values. Nonbelievers and people of doubt may not have much knowledge of the Scripture, but they can easily identify ungodly behaviors. These observations make it difficult for them to gain confidence in God, which makes it almost impossible for them to activate faith.

CHAPTER SUMMARY

Understanding the relationship between confidence and faith is critical for spiritual development. God has given a measure of faith to us all and our job is to activate our faith. Contrarily, we must learn confidence. Without confidence and faith, we lack hope and are full of doubt. Our minds are used to and prefer cause-and-effect logic, the logic system that scientists and scholars depend on. Faith is not logical and requires that we believe what we do not see.

Because the mind cannot see the faith that moves God, it rejects it. Therefore, nonbelievers must lean toward confidence in the earthly realm to activate faith in the spiritual realm. Because the natural mind tends to trust those things that have led to success in the past, people of doubt must first have the confidence to approach God in order to experience the effect of faith; they must be able to "see" effective outcomes. This is one reason why believers must present Christ in an observable, physical form. We must allow what is spiritual to manifest into flesh. Believers must become that fleshly image. We must demonstrate Christ through our behaviors. We do this by allowing Him to use our physical beings to represent His Sprit. God uses us to provide confidence to nonbelievers by renewing our minds, sharing His Spirit, and digesting his Word.

REFLECTION AND DISCUSSION QUESTIONS:

- Jot down what you believe was most meaningful from this chapter—something that you will share with a friend or colleague.
- How is this chapter relevant to your experiences in life?
- What "aha" moments did you have while reading this chapter?
- Reflect on Bobby's story. According to this chapter, what prevented him from writing a book?
- According to this chapter, why does the natural mind struggle with living by faith?
- What is one thing you will change or reflect on more after having read this chapter?

SCRIPTURE TO REFLECT ON:
I JOHN 5:14-15

This is the confidence we have in approaching God: that if we ask anything according to His will, He hears us. And if we know He hears us— whatever we ask—we know that we have what we asked of Him.

WHAT'S NEXT?

In the next chapter, I explain the importance and power in meditation. Success in every area of our life deals fundamentally with what we meditate about.

CHAPTER FIVE:
IMPORTANCE OF MEDITATION
IN SPIRITUAL DEVELOPMENT

When I remember You on my bed, I meditate on You in the night watches. Because You have been my help, therefore in the shadow of Your wings I will rejoice.

Psalms 63: 6-7, NKJV

During August of 2015, while at the Illinois State Fair, in Springfield, Illinois, I received an email from the president of an organization in Florida. The president of this organization shared that her board selected me, among other candidates, as the keynote speaker for a conference that would take place in June of 2016. The president inquired about my fees, my availability, and my willingness to speak at their conference. After learning about the terms and conditions of this conference, I agreed to join them and eventually flew out to Bonita, Florida, where the conference was held.

When I arrived at the hotel, on June 12, 2016, I checked in and immediately went to my room; while in my room, I unpacked my bags, hung my suit in the closet, showered, and prepared to meet the president who invited me to the conference. On my walk down to meet the president, I stopped by the Starbucks shop that was within the hotel and ordered a Venti Blonde coffee. While the young lady prepared my coffee, I turned around to see what was showing on the screen television, at which point I immediately became heartbroken—I began to pray in response to what I had read on the screen: "BREAKING NEWS: 49 People Dead in Orlando Night Club Massacre!"

The nation was just informed that a heavily armed gunman entered Pulse, a popular gay bar in Orlando, Florida, where he committed a massacre. The shooter's name was Omar Mateen. Days after the massacre, authorities learned that Omar had paid his entry fee to enter the bar, obtained a wrist band, and was present in the club prior to returning to take the lives of others.

An important question is, what prompted Omar to engage in what is now described as the "deadliest mass shooting by a single gunman" and "deadliest incident of violence against LGBT people in U.S. history"? Although no one may know how Omar truly felt prior to returning to Pulse to execute his attack, there is one thing that we could state with confidence, and that is Omar meditated. He meditated to take the lives of others in a violent and disturbing way. At some point—and perhaps over time—Omar engaged in deep meditation, which led to killing 49 people and being killed by Florida police.

THE POWER IN MEDITATION

When was the last time you were in a moment of deep meditation? What did you do directly after your meditation? How did you feel? Exhilarated? Fearful? Angry? Depressed? Anxious? Afraid?

When we meditate on a particular idea, our physiological systems generate chemical responses that affect our moods and behaviors. For example, as a result of our mediation, we often

- create innovative discoveries,
- work through difficult problems,
- live out fantasies,
- solve some unknown,
- give up,
- lose faith,
- commit horrific crimes,
- doubt God.

And by meditation, we are motivated to either obey or disobey. Meditation is a mental activity that affects our attitudes, moods, behaviors, and spiritual development.

May the arrogant be put to shame for wronging me without cause; but I will meditate on Your precepts.

Psalms 119:78

Many people associate the word *meditation* with Eastern religious practices or think in terms of stress-reduction exercises. But meditation actually refers to a range of behaviors and is a daily ritual for all humans. When we concentrate, contemplate, or ponder specific matters, we engage in moments of meditation; consequently, our mood, attitude, and behavior reflect these meditative experiences.

MEDITATION

Meditation is a process of reflecting on a specific issue. During meditation, the mind is carefully gathering thoughts and ideas. Confronting demands of society with limited time, we must learn to meditate on what matters most. This means we must focus our attention and thoughts on the things that develop our minds and spirits. Therefore, meditation is our key to manipulating personal burdens. But, as described in Omar's experience, meditation could also lead to destruction.

Now that you understand that meditation is a process of focusing your ideas, ask yourself this: What usually consumes my thoughts? Although it is a powerful ability, many people refuse to meditate or consider fully their thoughts, and the consequences of their actions, prior to acting. Consequently, they make poor, impulsive decisions. Contrarily, many people continually find themselves under pressure and stressed, because they prepare for the upcoming week, month, and year, but neglect daily preparation. Upon waking in the morning, we should ponder the many things that we must accomplish that given day and decide which of our tasks are most important.

Making a mental note is often difficult to remember because of the extensive demands of life. Instead of depending on mental notes, simply jot down what you need to accomplish that particular day and actively work to complete all objectives. How will we ever plan for a successful future if we cannot plan a 24-hour day? In order to develop mentally and spiritually, it is essential that we meditate on things that can improve our lives.

THE POWER IN THOUGHT

When I give you the go-ahead, put this book aside and take a couple of minutes to jot down the things that consume your daily meditation. Take a moment to think about thoughts that usually cross your mind. What do you find yourself concentrating on throughout the course of a day? Don't proceed with the reading until you have jotted down your daily thoughts. If you find that your meditations are personal, simply write them down and after you have read this chapter, shred the paper that lists your thoughts. The purpose is to put your thoughts on paper so you can actually see what is consuming your mind, and thus, controlling your emotions and your life. Are you ready? Go!

Now that you've jotted down the things that consume your mind, review them to see if they are positive, negative, or a reflection of both positive and negative thoughts? When we understand what is consuming our thoughts, we will have a better understanding of our moods and dispositions. For instance, if we notice that we are always thinking about and struggling with the demands of being a single parent, our behaviors and moods will reflect our contemplation. If we meditate on how intractable social problems appear to be, we will develop negative views of life; consequently, negativity and doubt will rule our minds. If we meditate on refuting the existence of God, our minds will tell us that Christ's experience at the cross is utter foolishness. If we have poor health and constantly meditate on our conditions, our thoughts will depress us and make our health conditions worse.

Contrarily, if we meditate on overcoming social problems, we will acquire optimistic attitudes. If we meditate on becoming successful, we will find hope. If we meditate on our ability to achieve, we will gain confidence. If we meditate on our ability to become wise, we will understand that knowledge is available to all. If we meditate on how our ideas frame our attitudes and behaviors, we will learn that positive ideas lead to joyous lives. We should not only meditate on positive thoughts, but also work to bring positive thoughts to life. Meditation brings about transformation! Meditation and transformation are interrelated components that will either facilitate or hinder our personal and spiritual growth.

In your anger do not sin; when you are on your beds, search your hearts and be silent.

Psalms 4:4

If you usually respond impulsively to anger, before reacting *automatically*, contemplate possible consequences and then remain silent. Psalms 4:4 is a perfect example of allowing God to transform your mind through meditation. After you have meditated on the potential consequences of impulsive actions, you should learn that retaliation is not always the best option. You could use this knowledge to transform your behaviors from impulsivity to humility.

MEDITATION: MENTAL MODELING

We learn behaviors from meditation. It is common to perceive our ideas as models and behave according to our thoughts. I call this phenomenon of learning behaviors through meditation *mental modeling,* because, in most cases, we believe our thoughts are perfect examples of how we should act; we consider them praiseworthy and most trusted. We validate our assumptions, because we seem to specialize in knowing how we feel *and* how others feel. We believe our thoughts are often accurate. The problem with depending on our ideas to understand other people is we often misinterpret behaviors. Actually, we are often horrible at interpreting other people's actions.

Mental models function similarly to role models we encounter in our daily lives. Thus, when we meditate on issues, our thoughts model a particular behavior, and we usually act out the mental activity. For example, when we meditate on retaliation, we are often motivated and influenced by our thoughts. We contemplate reasons why we should retaliate. At the end of the day, we find ourselves thinking, "God, I shouldn't have done that! I shouldn't have treated them like that." If we are sensitive to conviction, we usually say something like, "I'm going to apologize" or "I'm going to try to fix that situation!"

When an individual commits suicide because of depression, what do you believe influences the actual suicidal act? The answer is meditation. Meditation is the influencing factor to a host of behaviors, including homicide, rape, and adultery. When an individual has concluded that God does not exist, meditation is responsible for molding such belief. Meditation is the influential factor when committing most behaviors, moral and immoral. Mark 7:20-23 makes this point clear:

> *What comes out of a man is what makes him 'unclean.' For from within, out of men's hearts, come evil thoughts, sexual immorality, theft, murder, adultery, greed, malice, deceit, lewdness, envy, slander, arrogance and folly. All these evils come from inside and make a man 'unclean.'*

Because our thoughts are often negative, mental modeling gives rise to intolerance. The problem lies in our minds. Although our ideas are usually full of error, many people believe their thoughts about other people are accurate.

NEGATIVE THOUGHTS

Negative thought patterns defile our earthly and spiritual lives. Instead of correcting them, we allow them to consume our minds. The Bible recommends that we meditate on information that will keep us in perfect peace rather than on ideas that will depress our spirits. Instead of relying on negative thinking and intuition to make decisions, Jesus recommends that we compare our thoughts to His thoughts. We understand His thoughts by reading and meditating on His Word. By thinking consistently with the Word, our ideas will resemble a perfect model.

Is there reason to believe our ideas can be trusted when we adopt the thoughts of God? Colossians 1:19-22 explains why Christ's thoughts are valid. It says,

> *"For God was pleased to have all His fullness dwell in Him, and through Him to reconcile to Himself all things, whether things on earth or things in heaven, by making peace through His blood, shed on the cross. Once you were alienated from God and were enemies in your minds because of your evil behavior. But now He has reconciled you by Christ's physical body through death to present you holy in His sight, without blemish and free from accusation."*

We can trust the model of Christ because He is God. His grace ensures optimism and His doctrine ensures life. If your mind does not produce hope, you are thinking and living as if Jesus Christ did not die on the cross for your victory. You will be able to remain victorious "[I]f you continue in your faith, established and firm, not moved from the hope held out in the gospel" (Colossians, 1:23). Colossians 1:23 illustrates the idea of meditation and transformation as it exhorts us to "continue in our faith." This is the consequence of meditating on Christ. The precursor is meditation in order to realize transformation.

MEDITATION: DEVELOPING A CHRIST-LIKE IDENTITY

Many people have been believers for years but find difficulty inheriting Christ-like identities. Christ guarantees transformed identities through His atonement, but transformations rarely manifest because people refuse to reflect on Christ's work at the cross.

If we read about Christ-like attributes, we will have knowledge of His identity. But understanding His identity will not change our lives. God restores us as we understand and believe in His finished work at the cross. Thus, we must study His existence, study why He descended from heaven, and study what His work means in our lives. We must not only study the Person of Christ, but also meditate on His ministry, which is love. Meditating expresses our zeal to know, understand, and attain knowledge.

- How can we attain a Christ-like identity characterized by love if we constantly contemplate dislike or hate?
- How can we inherit Christ's humility if we feed on impulsivity?
- How can we acquire a peaceful personality if chaos gratifies us?

If you can admit that you engage in behaviors that are contrary to God's Word and admit that you need help with these behaviors, you will come closer to attaining a Christ-like identity than people who have been believers for years, but refuse to admit their weaknesses.

STRENGTHENING WEAKNESSES: GOING FROM NEGATIVE TO POSITIVE

How can we meditate and pray to God about our weaknesses if we don't have any weaknesses? What amazes me is nowadays when people have weaknesses, they train their minds to believe they have no weaknesses. Rather, they perceive the weakness as a less-strong point and then meditatively influence themselves to believe they have no weaknesses, only areas that are less strong than other areas. This thought pattern appears to be optimistic, but if we turn our weaknesses into less-strong points, we no longer have weaknesses. We are more prone to correcting weaknesses than less-strong points, because we think of less-strong points as almost strong. Being almost strong is not bad.

I believe one thing God despises is our tendency to *deny* weaknesses; in many instances, we refuse to repent, because we believe we do not have weaknesses. Consequently, we remain unchanged. The literal meaning of repentance is to *change the mind.* Because we often refuse to acknowledge our weaknesses, many of us do not allow God to change our minds. We remain in a destitute state. James 3:2 says, "We all stumble in many ways. If anyone is never at fault in what he says, he is a perfect man, able to keep his whole body in check." The more we deny our weaknesses, the more imperfect and destitute we become.

We naturally glorify our strengths and minimize our weaknesses. But if our desire is to mature mentally, emotionally, and spiritually, we must accurately identify our weaknesses so God can transform them into strengths. Our goal should be to imitate Paul in his confidence in God. Unlike Paul, some of us condemn ourselves because of our sins and because we have offended people for years. Instead of condemning himself for past behaviors, Paul looked toward heaven. He delighted in his weaknesses. Although he tortured and killed many believers in his day, he was bold enough to say,

[F]or my power is made perfect in weakness. Therefore, I will boast all the more gladly about my weakness, so that Christ's power may rest on me. That is why, for Christ's sake, I delight in weaknesses, in insults, in hardships, in persecutions, in difficulties. For when I am weak, then I am strong.

II Corinthians 12:9-10

So, do you say that you have weaknesses? Great! Which weaknesses are you struggling with?
- Negative self-image?
- Low self-esteem?
- Low self-confidence?
- Lack of competence?
- Lack of knowledge?
- Stinginess?
- Addiction?
- Pessimistic views of life?

Once you have consciously identified your weaknesses, plan to stop beating yourself over the head with them and instead, as Paul did, boast all the more gladly. What you should realize is, by God's grace, your mental strength is already made perfect, even in the midst of your weaknesses. You must have this confidence and faith in God. How you use this knowledge reflects the activity of your faith.

It is unlike human nature to rejoice because of weaknesses and hardships. But the rejoicing process does not represent praise of our weaknesses. Instead, we praise God, because He empowers us and provides strength during times of both weak and strong. Because God is all-powerful and He created us after His likeness, we have access to power. This power is not limited to physical strength, but also mental and spiritual power, even though at times we may feel weak.

I praise God for allowing us to boast and stand tall in His glory. In fact, since God's grace is sufficient and has already made us strong, gaining confidence and all other positive attributes depend on our faithfulness to actively release ourselves from such negativity. Faith and action are the prerequisites.

> *Not that I have already attained all this, or have already been made perfect, but I press on to take hold of that for which Christ Jesus took hold of me. Brothers, I do not consider myself yet to have taken hold of it. But one thing I do: Forgetting what is behind and straining toward what is ahead, I press on toward the goal to win the prize for which God has called me heavenward in Christ Jesus. All of us who are mature should take such a view of things. And if on some point you think differently, that too God will make clear to you. Only let us live up to what we have already attained.*

> Philippians 3:12-16

BECOMING SUSCEPTIBLE TO CHRIST'S IDENTITY

The key to Paul's message is in Philippians 3, verse 16, which states, "Only let us live up to what we have already attained." If we live up to what we have already attained, or learned, we will become more susceptible to Christ's identity. This means living up to what God has revealed to us through His Word. It does not mean trying to live like

Pastor Righteousness or Evangelist Holiness. We become susceptible by reading His Word to understand His thoughts and behaviors, and then by incorporating the knowledge with what we already know. But how can we meditate on God if we don't have any memory of His work, mission, or vision? We can't.

Paul understood he was not perfect. He kept working toward the day he would fulfill his purpose. That purpose was becoming all that he could become through Christ Jesus.

> *Therefore prepare your minds for action; be self-controlled; set your hope fully on the grace to be given you when Jesus Christ is revealed. As obedient children, do not conform to the evil desires you had when you lived in ignorance. But just as He who called you is holy, so be holy in all you do; for it is written: "Be holy, because I am holy."*

I Peter 1:13-16

Along with meditating on the truths that we have already learned, let's begin to contemplate about thinking clearly and exercising self-control. Let's meditate on obeying God, not for the purpose of being blessed, but simply because we are His children. When we find ourselves reverting to old, negative ways, let's ponder the fact that we are more knowledgeable now compared to when we committed sinful acts habitually. You are now more knowledgeable today than you were yesterday about spiritual perspectives. Let's challenge ourselves by becoming holy in everything we do because our Father said, "We must be holy because He is holy."

YOU ARE INVITED, AND IT'S FREE

I am committing fifteen minutes of my day to meditating on Christ. You are invited; will you join me? If you believe you do not know enough about Christ to meditate on Him, simply meditate on what you have learned thus far from reading this book. Philippians 3:16 says to live according to what you have already attained.

Together, as our spirits glorify God, we will meditate on who He is and what He has done for our lives. We will meditate on the fact that He has provided salvation and grace. We will meditate on His creations and on His attributes, which are the fruits of the Spirit: love, joy, peace, patience, kindness, goodness, faithfulness, gentleness, and self-control (Galatians 5:22-23). We will meditate on knowing God has a plan for our lives. We will meditate on how He allowed us to attain a truth that supersedes all doubt.

Not only will you and I glorify God through meditation, but other readers who also decide to participate in this meditative praise will add to our mental worship. Our meditation is not a 15-minute prayer. It is a sole concentration on Jesus Christ. By meditating on God, meditating on His wonderful attributes, we allow our minds to focus on His greatness, His sovereignty. Our meditation is consistent with Psalm 105:4, which exhorts us to "Look to the Lord and His strength; seek His face always."

By joining me in meditating on Jesus Christ daily, I am convinced that through faith, you will access all that is within your storehouse—all that God has set aside for you. Joining me in meditation exemplifies a determination and sentiment that expresses your fervor to experience Christ. May God bless you; your manifestation is on the way. I leave you with an important message:

> *Finally, brothers, whatever is true, whatever is noble, whatever is right, whatever is pure, whatever is lovely, whatever is admirable—if anything is excellent or praiseworthy—think about such things. Whatever you have learned or received or heard from me, or seen in me—put it into practice. And the God of peace will be with you.*

> Philippians 4:8-9

CHAPTER SUMMARY

When you think of the word *meditation*, what comes to your mind? What does this word mean? Many people associate the word meditation with Eastern religious practices or think in terms of stress-reduction exercises. But meditation actually refers to a range of behaviors and is a daily ritual for all humans. Meditation is simply a process of directing our thoughts on a particular thing or idea. Therefore, when we concentrate, contemplate, or ponder specific matters, we actually experience moments of meditation.

Meditation is a powerful mental ability, so powerful that our moods and attitudes reflect the things that we meditate. If we meditate on accomplishing our goals, pursuing a career, and being successful in every area of our life, we will have a positive outlook towards life and maintain optimistic attitudes. If we meditate on failing, having some disability, low skills, and being a single parent, then our moods will reflect our thoughts; we will have a negative outlook towards life and maintain pessimistic attitudes. Our moods and attitudes reflect the things that we meditate. In this chapter, I invite you to join me in a 15-minute daily meditation about Jesus Christ. Will you join me?

REFLECTION AND DISCUSSION QUESTIONS:

- Jot down what you believe was most meaningful from this chapter—something that you will share with a friend or colleague.
- How is this chapter relevant to your experiences in life?
- What "aha" moments did you have while reading this chapter?
- Reflect on the things that you think about daily. Jot these things down if you did not do it during the chapter reading.
- How often do you meditate on becoming successful and achieving your goals?
- What is one thing you will change or reflect on more after having read this chapter?

SCRIPTURE TO REFLECT ON:
PHILIPPIANS 4:8-9

Finally, brothers, whatever is true, whatever is noble, whatever is right, whatever is pure, whatever is lovely, whatever is admirable—if anything is excellent or praiseworthy—think about such things. Whatever you have learned or received or heard from me, or seen in me—put it into practice. And the God of peace will be with you.

WHAT'S NEXT?

In the next chapter, I discuss the purpose of memory in spiritual development. The most important concept of the next chapter is if you do not have memory of God's Word, it will be impossible to see Him carrying you through your storms. Consequently, you may feel that you are alone when experiencing trials and tribulations. You may feel as if God has forsaken you. Memory is a mental tool that we use to develop spiritually and to obtain the resources in our storehouse!

CHAPTER SIX:
THE PURPOSE OF MEMORY IN SPIRITUAL DEVELOPMENT

*Moreover, brethren, I declare unto you the gospel which I
preached unto you, which also ye have received, and wherein
ye stand; By which also ye are saved, if ye keep in memory what
I preach unto you, unless ye have believed in vain.*

I Corinthians 15:1-2, KJV

D
o you ever reflect on the promises that God has revealed to
you about your life? Have you kept these experiences in your
memory? Now that I am an adult, I often reflect on many of the
things God shared with me about my life and purpose. Although I have
retained in memory many stories and experiences that God has shared
with me, I often reflect on a time when I had an out of body experience.
An out of body experience is a situation where people experience the
world from a location outside of their physical bodies. I recall having this
experience when I was in middle school. I recall that, when I would retell
this experience, I could never finish the story without crying profusely
and being overwhelmed with emotions. I recall that the mere thought
of the experience would bring me to tears. I'll share this experience with
you.

One night as I prepared for bed, I did my usual routine. I showered,
brushed my teeth, cleaned my room, turned off the lights, and closed the
door. I slept best when my room was pitch dark. I slept in a twin bed, and
lay in the middle of the bed, with room on both the left and right side
of my body. This particular night, as I slept in the pitch-dark room, my
spirit left my body and settled in the top left corner of the room, next to

the closed door. When my spirit left my body, my consciousness was with my spirit; that is, it was through my spirit that I saw my body laying on the bed; it was through my spirit that I perceived the entire experience.

As I stared at my body, I observed an angel appear in my room, in the corner, directly to the left of where my body was positioned. The angel appeared in the corner, then, within a blink of an eye, transitioned from the corner to the right side of my body; it was as if I left just enough space for her body. When she laid next to me, she had a notepad and pen in her hand. She spoke to my body and said this: "You will make these many numbers . . ." She then wrote "200, 200, 200, 200, 200, 200, 200, 200, 200, 200, 200, 200, 200, 200, 200 . . . ." She wrote the number 200 on every line of the paper until she ran out of space. As she spoke to my body and wrote on the notepad, I watched her from the corner of my room. What was interesting was, although the room was pitch dark, the angel and the space where I laid was lit—as if a bright light hovered over that portion of my bed. After she spoke to my body and wrote on the pad, she disappeared, and my spirit immediately returned to my body.

When my spirit returned to my body, I laid in the bed, in the pitch dark room, and cried incessantly; tears flowed from my eyes like a river. I was terrified. I recall having chills all over my body. My heart felt as if it was about to burst through my chest. I eventually rushed out of my room and woke my mother up to share this incredible experience. I was unable to share the story with her initially, because I could not stop crying. My mother was able to calm me down at which point I shared the story with her. I recall sitting on the couch with her, on Jefferson Street, in Carpentersville, Illinois, where we contemplated what the "200" might have meant. My mother and I often talk about this experience and discuss what the 200 might mean for me as an adult. Interestingly, when I would share this story, as I grew older, I would cry in the same fashion that I cried as a kid. Retelling the story always brought me back to the corner of my room, on Jefferson Street, where I watched my body lay on the bed, next to this angel.

I remember this story vividly and my ability to recall and retell this story—which happened over 20 years ago—sheds a light on a mental tool that is vital to spiritual development. That mental tool is *memory*.

Important questions about memory are the following:

- What is the purpose of memory in spiritual development?
- Why did God create our minds with the ability to remember information?
- Why does Scripture advise us to keep certain promises within memory?
- How would life be if we could not remember information?
- How might memory allow us to access what God has for us?
- What role does memory play in identifying our purpose?
- How might memory assist with achieving success in every area of our life?

MEMORY IN A SPIRITUAL LIFE

Memory is the process of reserving information acquired from experiences, which we use to understand our present life. When we first encounter information, if we process and store the information, we'll be able to use it to solve problems in the future. Thus, our memories are mental tools that we use to construct images. Mental images—memories—help us create ideas and knowledge.

Without memory, spiritual development would be impossible. We would not be able to store information about God's Word. Because of memory, when we study God's Word and His promises, we are able to store the information with our personal experiences. In other words, we're able to project mental images of God's Word carrying us through our storms. We're able to do so only when we have memorized His Word.

Many people find it difficult to renew their minds, because their memories do not reflect Christ's finished work at the cross. Their memories do not project an accurate description of grace, and consequently, they believe living for Christ is impossible. Others find it difficult to renew their minds, because *Jesus Christ* is a simple idea to them, as opposed to a mental image; their knowledge of Jesus Christ is limited to a mere concept. This means their memories of Christ have yet to transition from a simple idea to a well-developed mental representation. Allow me to differentiate between concepts and mental representations to fully appreciate this idea.

CONCEPTS AND MENTAL REPRESENTATIONS

A *concept* is simply a general idea of something. You may have formed a variety of concepts or ideas about what you have read in this book thus far. We create ideas or concepts for just about everything we encounter. In fact, our present knowledge of life is a host of basic ideas to which our minds have provided meaning. Our minds sort and categorize information so our ideas will have context and will become more meaningful. Because of the mind's ability to sort and arrange information, ideas aren't just floating around freely in our heads. Instead, our minds create mental images or representations from our ideas.

I'll illustrate the process of transforming ideas into mental representations. Let's use, for example, reading development. Babies can't read because of their inability to provide meaning to letters, along with various other factors that pertain to brain and language development. As they develop, are exposed to print, and learn letter recognition, their minds will develop *ideas* for letters. For example, have you ever heard children learning their letters say, "Mommy, Daddy, that's a letter A, right?" At this point, they have transitioned from perceiving simple *lines*, to providing a more advanced meaning—*a letter A.* Once they learn a single letter, their minds form *mental representations* or *images* for that letter; anything that looks like the letter *A* to them, children at that stage will call an *A*.

Once children learn the entire alphabet and master phonics and phonemic awareness, they will finally understand that each letter produces a particular sound to form a word. Print is more meaningful to children when they come to the knowledge that "letters talk"—that each letter has a corresponding sound—and combine to form words. Children eventually create letter-sound relationships in their minds and memorize words they are most familiar with. From this process, they are able to recall alphabetical relationships; they are able to pull images of letters and sounds from their memories when required to read. They become fluent readers by reading daily and memorizing words they can identify upon sight—without having to sound them out. Fluent readers are able to read with speed and accuracy.

I'll use a different example, one you may be experiencing as you are reading this book. If this is your first time reading about human behaviors, the mind, and spiritual development, your mind is currently adjusting to the concepts, which are the ideas present in this book. As you read, your mind processes the ideas. Once you process the information, you will begin to make judgments about the ideas present in this book; you will begin to determine if the ideas you are reading are true or false. From this process, you may say to yourself, "Yes, I agree with that," or "No, I disagree!" Eventually, through repeated exposure, your mind will consume the information in this book and produce a mental structure—a meaningful representation of what you are reading. When this happens, you will have memorized, to a certain extent, what you are reading.

Essentially, when we create ideas, we use past experiences to understand them. If our minds were unable to formulate mental pictures of experiences and ideas, we would have no memory and would be unable to access information we learned in the past. If this were the case, every experience would be new and rare. We would be unable to identify our relatives, and literally, everything we perceive would be unusual!

CREATING MENTAL IMAGES OF CHRIST

When you think about *Christ, grace*, and *salvation,* what comes to your mind? Do you experience a feeling of reassurance in your spiritual walk when you hear these terms? When you think about grace, do you feel confident in your salvation? The answers to these questions will allow you to understand your mind's ideas or mental images of Christ and His work at the cross.

If meditating on Christ and His work at the cross doesn't resonate peace in your mind, chances are you may not truly understand what His work means in your life. Upon hearing the name Jesus Christ, our minds begin to project ideas or images about Him. These ideas or images are memories. We usually feel a certain way about the memories our minds reveal to us. For example, if you do not believe in Christ's existence, your mind will reveal memories that explain why you believe Christ is some make-believe character. In addition, your mind will have attached feelings to these memories and ideas. Consequently, upon hearing the name Jesus Christ, your mind will automatically project feelings of some make-believe character, as opposed to projecting salvation and grace. If you believe Christ has let you down on numerous occasions, your mind will reveal these memories and your feelings about Christ will reflect the mental image you had once created about Christ. If this represents your mental image of Christ, your mind will project negative thoughts upon hearing His name or seeing His name written in books.

In the same manner, if you believe in the existence of Christ and believe He is God, your mind will reveal memories or images of His glory. Your mind will project memories of His crucifixion and grace. If you believe in Christ's existence and are familiar with His work at the cross, your mind will have memorized His proclamation, "It is finished!" Your perception of trials and tribulations will reflect this knowledge, as opposed to reflecting trials you may be experiencing. Your memories will reflect the knowledge of Christ based on biblical and personal experiences in your life. Your faith will have allowed you to interpret the move of God's hand during your hardship. For example, the author of Psalm 116:1-2 expresses his mental images of God: "I love the Lord, for He heard my cry; He heard my cry for mercy. Because He turned His ear to me, I will call on Him as long as I live." When you think about something that is gratifying and pleasurable, your body usually gets aroused, because your mind has a mental image that includes the *thing* and your body's reaction to it.

A more earthly example of mental images is winning the lottery. Most people will get emotionally aroused if they have purchased a winning lottery ticket. They'll get aroused, because their minds have formed an image of the lottery, the amount of money the lottery offers, and the fact that winning the lottery will allow them to buy items that will satisfy their desires. If winning the lottery were merely a concept to them, a simple idea, chances are they would not get aroused or react similarly to someone who has an actual image of winning the lottery.

The difference between forming an idea and forming a mental image is that an idea is usually not well developed. To develop ideas, one has to think through the idea, consider the idea within the context of other meaningful information, and contemplate the benefits and consequences the idea may present. A mental image is a result of thinking through a concept and understanding an idea in relation to other meaningful information. We react to mental images, because we understand the benefits and consequences they present. This is why the author of Psalm 116:1-2 proclaimed, "I love the Lord, for He heard my voice; He heard my cry for mercy."

Now that you can differentiate between simple ideas and mental images, I'll ask the question again. When you think about Christ, grace, and salvation, what comes to your mind? If your thoughts don't reflect reassurance, confidence, or peace when you think about Jesus, salvation, and grace, it could be that the names are only concepts to you and have not transitioned into meaningful images.

It is possible that you have categorized Jesus with other terms such as Christianity, religion, and spirituality. If so, Christ and His work at the cross probably do not move you; your thoughts of Christ are probably no different from your thoughts of Christianity, religion, and spirituality. The reality is the *Person* of Christ is actually God. Christ's existence is much greater than our ideas of Christianity, religion, and spirituality.

On the other hand, many people aren't moved when thinking about Christ, because they had at one point created mental images of His glory and salvation, but later in life—for some reason—lost faith in these same beliefs. Their mental representations of Christ either placed them into a depressive state, because they believed and felt that God failed them, or the thought of Christ had no effect on their being, positive or negative. Similarly, if you reject the existence of Christ, you will eventually develop mental representations of Him that will produce oppositional faith.

Our walk with God is not about feelings, however, and we should never qualify or quantify our walk with God based on our emotions. In other words, we shouldn't let our feelings determine our faith. Although our feelings are unimportant in regards to faith, they do allow us to know whether we have become complacent in our walk with God. The reality is we must create mental images of Christ that will allow us to persevere, no matter how we feel. If we don't read the Bible to learn about Christ's experiences on earth, our idea about Him will remain an idea, it will never reach a mental picture.

> *By this gospel you are saved, if you hold firmly to the word I preached to you. Otherwise, you have believed in vain. For what I received I passed on to you as of first importance: that Christ died for our sins according to the Scriptures, that He was buried, that He was raised on the third day according to the Scriptures, and that He appeared to Peter, and then to the Twelve [apostles]. After that, He appeared to more than five hundred of the brothers at the same time, most of whom are still living, though some have fallen asleep. Then He appeared to James, then to all the apostles, and last of all He appeared to me also, as to one abnormally born.*

> I Corinthians 15:2-8

If you lack memory of Jesus Christ, you will lack knowledge about His work, ministry, and purpose. It's a blessing that you're seeking to understand human behaviors from a spiritual perspective, but if you don't allow your mind to transform this knowledge into mental images, you will only conceptualize, or *make ideas* about what you are reading. The Bible says that we are transformed by the renewing of our minds (Romans 12:2), not by simply creating ideas about the Word of God.

Transforming our minds requires believing in God's Word. From studying and believing in His Word, we are able to store His promises. For example, He says, "If any man is in Christ, he is a new creation, the old has gone and the new has come" (II Corinthians 5:17).

Based on this promise, you should know that God recreates you when you accept the Lord as your Savior. When I say that God recreates you, I mean that He restores your mind with His Spirit. Your job is to dig deep into His Word to understand what *a new creation* means and create memories that show God working on your behalf!

The fact is God has already worked in our favor, in every area of our lives. But because many people have not created mental images of His Word and do not understand how He operates, they do not experience His blessings and promises. Even worse, they do not identify Him as their provider. We should not only create memories of Christ working on our behalf, but also learn godly behaviors as our minds paint mental images of His finished work at the cross.

If you believe God's Word is true, no matter what you experience in life, your memories will continue to reflect reverence for God. This means you will continue to honor, respect, and worship Him despite your trials and tribulations. This idea does not mean you will never have questions about why certain things happen in life as they do, and it does not mean you will never feel that God has left you. What it does mean, however, is when you begin to feel that God has abandoned you, the Holy Spirit will comfort you and bring serenity to your mind, even during times of hardship.

Your faith will determine how long it will take for you to experience God's comfort in times of hardship, in that all that you will ever need in your life is provided through God's experience at the cross. He has already paid the price through the shedding of His blood. We experience His work through faith, by believing that He has already worked on our behalf—no matter what we experience in the present moment. We are able to reverence God in the midst of our trials when we create memories of His faithfulness. This idea makes me think about the life of Job.

Satan took Job from the pinnacle of prosperity to the depths of poverty. Job lost his property and, even worse, his children. Satan struck Job with painful boils all over his body. From the torment he experienced, Job's wife told him to "Curse God and die!" (Job 2:9, NKJV).

In response to his wife's statement, Job said, "You speak as one of the foolish women speaks. Shall we indeed accept good from God, and shall we not accept adversity?" (Job 2:10, NKJV). The Bible shows that, unlike his wife, Job had created mental images of God that allowed him to persevere through hardship.

MEMORY: UNDERSTANDING SATAN'S DECEPTION

For we do not wrestle against flesh and blood, but against principalities, against powers, against the rulers of the darkness of this age, against spiritual hosts of wickedness in the heavenly places.

Ephesians 6:12, NKJV

If you ask a group of people how their day or week has went, it is possible to hear the following responses:

- "It's been tough, but I made it through"
- "I haven't been feeling well, but I've been able to recover"
- "My job has been getting the best of me"
- "Well, I lost my job but I'm still living"

These responses reveal that evil forces bombard us daily. These forces are not visible to the human eye but work through people to steal our joy. Consequently, many people are continually backed into corners, because they believe they lack power to speak life into their lives. Memory allows us to know that we can call on the name of the Lord for strength, in good and bad times.

If we were unable to remember what the Scriptures proclaim about Christ, the ills of this world would consume us. In fact, many people are consumed emotionally, because their mental images do not reflect the Word of God. Their mental images reflect a god of torture, a god that sits around condemning them and others. Because they have not gained confidence and faith in God, these people attempt to wrestle against principalities and against wicked powers using their human abilities and limited knowledge. We describe social and economical problems— violence, social ills, recession—as our earthly minds understand them. We describe them as worldly ills. The Bible describes these experiences as fighting against rulers of the darkness of this age. In other words, the Bible tells us that what we experience in the natural realm is actually something happening in the spiritual realm.

Why do you believe the adversary and his forces continually bombard our lives? Ultimately, Satan tries to get us to focus on his obstacles in exchange for our memory of the Scriptures. If we focus on the trials that the adversary prepares before us, we'll never remember what the Word teaches about temptations and perseverance. Satan's main objective is to get us to forget about the existence of God. When He puts trials and tribulations before you, don't exchange your memory of Scripture for His obstacles. Instead, remember, *you serve a risen Savior!*

Memory allows us to decipher Satan's deception. Although we have the ability to recall the deceptive works of the adversary and his army, many of us continue to fall into the same traps. We forget how he once deceived us. This idea reminds me of the *Tom and Jerry* cartoon show.

Whenever Tom deceived Jerry, Jerry used the deception as a teachable moment. Jerry was often able to avoid Tom's tricks, because he was familiar with Tom's strategies; he understood Tom's motives. Although Jerry learned from one situation, Tom prepared subsequent traps to attempt to destroy him.

If you happen to fall in your spiritual walk, allow the fall to be a teachable moment. Learn from the fall. If you continue to forget how you were deceived in the past, you will continue to be deceived in the future.

THE OUTCOME OF *Perseverance:* THE KEY TO SUCCESS

There's good news about being tempted if you utilize the power of memory. After you endure trials of temptations, you'll be equipped with a message. To avoid this glorious ending point of tribulation, the enemy tries to destroy you physically, mentally, emotionally, and spiritually. The adversary understands that if you persevere through your storm, you will have access to memory that outlines his tactics. He also understands that your memory has the potential to inspire perseverance and strengthen others. When another person is going through the same struggle you experienced, or if someone reverts to sinful behaviors, you can stand firmly and proclaim,

The devil comes to deceive. He does his dirt then paints a picture of Jesus in your mind as the accuser. If you believe God set you up for failure, your mind will recall mental images of how God let you down, which will eventually hinder your development. Don't let this happen. One thing you must store in your memory is this:

Don't be deceived, my dear brothers. Every good and perfect gift is from above, coming down from the Father of the heavenly lights, who does not change like shifting shadows.

> *He chose to give us birth through the word of truth, that we may be a kind of first–fruits of all He created.*

James 1:16–18

USING MEMORY TO ADVANCE THE KINGDOM

If we are to renew our minds, it's imperative that we memorize God's Word. This is God's ultimate reason for equipping our minds with the ability to memorize information. God did not create our minds with the ability to build mental representations so that we could create memories of nonsense. In today's world, unfortunately, people are using their minds to create a vast amount of nonsense and nonproductive knowledge; they are constantly creating new memories that will not develop them spiritually. Knowledge that does not lead to salvation through Christ will someday be of no use.

Understanding the usefulness of memory, we must look inward and question ourselves about our memory of God and His work at the cross.

Currently, what memories do you have about Jesus Christ that will allow you to come out of the traps you are in or the traps that await you?

What memory about Jesus Christ do you have that can pull you out if you happen to fall into a trap?

It is great to be able to dig deep into the Word and pray when you fall short, but it is even better to have the Word inside of you, speaking out when confronted by obstacles!

Many people have heard the history of Jesus Christ but do not understand His glory. The reason is they have no mental representation or holding place for His existence. Let's remember Christ's purpose for coming to earth. Let's remember how epoch–making His crucifixion was. Let's remember why it was important that Jesus did not succumb to the temptations of the devil when He fasted forty days and forty nights. Let's remember that everything Jesus did on earth was done to redeem humankind of their sins and also to set the tone for our new lives. Let's remember that all that God did in the natural world was done to provide examples of how we should worship Him in spirit.

Let's take advantage of knowledge that leads to success in every area of our lives, success that was predetermined when God stated,

Let Us make man in Our image, in Our likeness.

Genesis 1:26

CHAPTER SUMMARY

Memory is the process of reserving information acquired from experiences, which we use to understand our present life. When we first encounter information, if we process and store the information, we'll be able to use it to solve problems in the future. Thus, our memories are mental tools that we use to construct images of the world. Without memory, spiritual development would be impossible; we would not be able to store information about God's Word, or remember His working on our behalf. Because of memory, when we study God's Word and His promises, we are able to store the information with our personal experiences.

In other words, we're able to project mental images of God's Word carrying us through our storms. We're able to project mental images of God's promises only when we have memorized His Word. Many people find it difficult to renew their minds because their memories do not reflect Christ's finished work at the cross. Their memories do not project an accurate description of grace, and consequently, they believe living for Christ is impossible.

REFLECTION AND DISCUSSION QUESTIONS:

- Jot down what you believe was most meaningful from this chapter—something that you will share with a friend or colleague.
- How is this chapter relevant to your experiences in life?
- What "aha" moments did you have while reading this chapter?
- Reflect on my out of body experience. Have you ever had a similar experience or know someone who has?
- What is the difference between an idea and a mental representation?
- Why does memory lead to spiritual development?
- What is one thing you will change or reflect on more after having read this chapter?

SCRIPTURE TO REFLECT ON:
I CORINTHIANS 15:1-2, KJV

Moreover, brethren, I declare unto you the gospel which I preached unto you, which also ye have received, and wherein ye stand; By which also ye are saved, if ye keep in memory what I preach unto you, unless ye have believed in vain.

WHAT'S NEXT?

In the next chapter, I reveal the importance of learning. Allowing the Spirit of God to renew our minds is one thing, but learning to abide in His will, according to the Word, is another. Often, people accept Christ into their lives, but fail to learn the ways of God and refuse to apply His principles to achieve success in their life. Simply renewing your mind will not provide you with knowledge of God's Word. *You must learn* to think like God and understand human behaviors from a spiritual perspective.

CHAPTER SEVEN:
Learning to Be Born Again

This is what the Lord says: "As for all My wicked neighbors who seize the inheritance I gave My people Israel, I will uproot them from their lands and I will uproot the house of Judah from among them. But after I uproot them, I will again have compassion and will bring each of them back to his own inheritance and his own country. And if they learn well the ways of My people and swear by My name, saying, 'As surely as the Lord lives'— even as they once taught My people to swear by Baal—then they will be established among My people. But if any nation does not listen, I will completely uproot and destroy it," declares the Lord.

Jeremiah 12:14–17

When was the last time you were required to learn a new skill, or the last time you had to learn cultural values that were drastically different from your own? The essence of my work as a school psychologist is helping students learn at their highest potential. As a school psychologist, I have a special interest and appreciation for learning and am often in awe at the intricacies that take place throughout the learning process. I spend countless hours integrating and applying psychological principles, educational theories, and research to help students learn new concepts and information.

When I first started studying psychology, many people attempted to protect my salvation by saying, "Dwayne, whatever you do, do not let psychology ruin your faith!" Ministers told me that science, including social sciences such as psychology, seeks to debunk Scripture and that I must not allow my interest in psychology to warp my mind. From studying psychology, I see clearly the importance of psychological processes, such as learning, in spiritual development.

For example, in Jeremiah 12:14-17, God warned the many nations who were plotting to inherit the blessings He released to Israel. He explained that He would uproot them from their own lands. What I find most interesting is, although these nations were plotting to seize the inheritance of Israel, God was willing to establish them among His people. Notice that God was not going to establish them among His people without their own effort. Establishing them among His people was contingent on an important factor: whether they learned His people's ways. Interestingly, God based His decision solely on their ability to *learn,* which involves psychological processes.

As shown throughout Scripture, and contrary to the warnings that I received from ministers and loved ones, Jesus places great emphases on psychology and psychological processes—such as thinking, believing, memory, and learning—and His decision to destroy the plotting nations if they did not learn, illustrates this point. Unfortunately, the ministers who warned me about studying psychology placed God in a box and only saw His creation within Scripture.

THE IMPORTANCE OF LEARNING IN SPIRITUAL DEVELOPMENT

Why is learning so meaningful to God? Like all mental attributes, learning is an ability that allows us to understand God's existence. Learning is the activity by which we use psychological processes to generate knowledge. We don't attain knowledge by simply skimming through a book or listening to a lecture. Instead, we acquire knowledge from studying, meditating, and seeking to understand information. Learning new information is what allows mental, emotional, and spiritual transformation.

Learning is an interesting process. Some people learn rather quickly, in a short span of time; others may learn more slowly and may require more time. The speed with which information is learned depends on the individual and the learning task. Although we vary in the speed with which we learn information, learning has the same effect on us all: It allows us to do things we were unable to do prior to our learning experience. This is why the Lord placed such a great demand on learning concerning the nations who were plotting against Israel. The Lord understood that their behaviors would destroy them unless they were willing to learn the customs and culture of His people.

In this chapter, I discuss learning and mental processes that help facilitate learning. After having read this chapter, you'll understand why God places great emphases on learning and studying to develop spiritually.

THE LEARNING PROCESS

The process of learning is intricate, yet amazing. Can you recall ever telling a child to stop writing on the walls or to stop sucking his or her thumbs? Have you tried to potty-train a child, or heard of the difficulty in potty training? While attempting to teach children certain behaviors, you may say to yourself, "I keep teaching this child, but he is not learning!" or "I keep putting this child on the stool, but she keeps reverting to wetting her pants!" Amazingly, one day you notice a complete change in the child's behavior. He is no longer writing on the walls of your home, but writing on paper; she is no longer wetting her pants, but running to the stool.

Although learning is an extremely difficult concept to define, I used the above examples to help illustrate the process. The examples show that we rarely learn difficult information upon our first time reading or hearing it. Rather, learning is a process that takes time. Learning requires us to rehearse, memorize, and attach information to some real or imagined reality. We must put information into some context so that our minds can provide meaning to it. This process may manifest early in the learning experience or may take weeks, months, or even years to manifest.

There are at least five reasons why people fail to demonstrate behaviors or knowledge they should have learned: either

1. they never learned the correct information—meaning, they learned the wrong information;
2. they forgot the information *immediately* after having learned it;

3. they learned the information at one point, but because they did not rehearse the information daily, their current knowledge, or the information they do rehearse daily, has replaced what they had learned previously;

4. they are *still learning,* and will not display or verbalize the information until their minds convert the knowledge into a mental image that he or she can fully understand; or

5. they have successfully learned the information, but *refuse* to verbalize, teach, or display it.

WHAT IS LEARNING?

How do you define learning? Social scientists who study how people learn are called *learning theorists.* They create ideas and theories based on their research about learning. The most accepted definition by learning theorists is that learning is "a relatively permanent change in behavior or in behavior potentiality that results from experience." One of the key words in the definition, I believe, is *relatively.*

What is meant by relatively? Relatively refers to the extent to which we compare one thing to another; or the extent to which something has a relationship to, a connection with, or a necessary dependence on something else. The term *relative* is used because it is impossible to know the merit of one thing unless it is compared to another. For example, rich and poor are relative terms. We do not know how rich or poor someone is unless they are compared to some index. In fact, almost everything we compare is dependent on something else. For example, we do not know how tall someone is unless we compare his or her height to others. I am tall relative to those who are much shorter than 5 feet 7 inches. Although I am generally considered short, my *shortness* depends on the height of others who are taller than I am. If I lived in a village with people who were all 5 feet 7 inches, I wouldn't know that the people in my village are short unless I met someone much taller than us.

Essentially, almost everything has a relationship to, a connection with, or a necessary dependence on something else. When we compare things to determine their value, we do so in relative terms. The *thing* that learning has a connection with, relationship to, and dependence on is experience. A *relatively* permanent change in behavior, then, is based on how often we experience the learned behavior. If we learn a behavior and incorporate the learned behavior in our daily lives, the behavior change will remain relatively stable. If we learn a new behavior but do not practice the behavior daily, the behavior will transition to nearly unlearned.

BEHAVIORAL CHANGE = LEARNING

According to learning theorists, a change in one's behavior is evidence that someone has experienced some type of learning. Based on this belief, when someone displays a change in behavior, from aggressive to mild mannered, for example, learning has taken place. In fact, learning theorists believe that many people demonstrate the same behavior over time, because they have not learned new information that leads to change.

Learning theorists believe learning must be observed through one's behavior, and this belief sets them apart from other theorists. I'll provide an example of what learning theorists mean when they say learning must be observed through behavior. If I explain to a student that 5 times 5 equals 25, but when I quiz him, he constantly tells me that 5 times 5 equals 10, then he shows, through his behaviors (responses), that he has not learned the mathematical concept.

If the student answers correctly by telling me that 5 times 5 equals 25, his behaviors indicate that he has learned the concept for that moment. The question now becomes how long will he know that 5 times 5 equals 25? A similar question is how long will he remember what he has learned? The answer is his learning would be based on experience or how often he practices the multiplication fact and how often he makes the concept a part of his everyday life. If he learns the concept and never thinks about it again, his learning would be relatively short; if he learns the concept and makes it a part of his everyday life, his learning would be relatively permanent.

Probably one of the most important aspects about learning, then, is how we perceive and store information. Thus, memory leads to learning. Since a *relatively permanent change* marks learning, if we are unable to remember information that brings about change, we will never learn, and according to learning theorists, it would be difficult to change our thoughts and behaviors.

To understand learning, it is helpful to focus on how we remember information. Cognitive psychologists—psychologists who study the way we think, learn, perceive, and remember information—focus on three main components to understand the phenomena of learning. These components include our ability to encode, store, and retrieve information. Although these operations have been associated more closely with memory, they are key factors to learning.

THREE INTERRELATED COMPONENTS THAT ASSIST LEARNING

Encode

Encoding is simply transforming information into an image and placing that image into memory. When we observe information, our minds attempt to make meaning of the information by converting it into meaningful images. If our minds were unable to translate an image or sound into an illustration, our perception—the image or sound— would remain meaningless. We would be unable to provide meaning to what we perceive. In fact, when we observe information that is unique to our experiences, it is often difficult for us to interpret it. For example, if you are monolingual, only speak English, the Spanish language may appear foreign to you. Likewise, if you speak and read English only, Sinography— the Chinese writing system—appears foreign to you. This is because you have not encoded a mental image that gives meaning to Chinese writing symbols.

Storage

Storage refers to our mind's ability to store encoded information. Just as we use an attic, garage, or basement to store items and belongings, our minds store information until we need it. For example, right now, you're probably not thinking about what you did yesterday if you are focusing your attention on learning the information you are reading. However, if someone interrupts your reading and asks you what you did yesterday, you would more than likely be able to recall something you did in the course of the day.

Retrieval

Retrieval is the cleanup operation: Information that was encoded and stored is retrievable when needed. Although you are automatically reading the words in this book, your mind is able to interpret each alphabetical letter and put together a word because of the retrieval process. Take for example the word *retrieval.* The term is actually nine individual letters put together to spell a word: r-e-t-r-i-e-v-a-l. Because your mind has encoded and stored the ability to read words fast and automatically, for example, instead of sounding out letters individually (r-e-t-r-i-e-v-a-l), you are able to read the entire word at once: *retrieval.* Your mind is able to pull from memory the sounds that make up the word retrieval.

Encoding, storing, and retrieving are interdependent components. What will happen if your mind encodes and stores the wrong information? When your mind retrieves, the information will be misleading. Likewise, what will happen if you don't properly store information? You will eventually forget the information.

GOD'S EMPHASIS ON LEARNING ACCURATE INFORMATION

Now that you understand the relationship between memory and learning, which includes encoding, storing, and retrieving information, let's reexamine what the Lord explained to the nations who were plotting against Israel. While you're reading, continue to ask yourself, "Why does God place such great emphasis on learning *accurate* information?"

This is what the Lord says:

> *As for all My wicked neighbors who seize the inheritance I*
> *gave My people Israel, I will uproot them from their lands and*
> *I will uproot the house of Judah from among them. But after*
> *I uproot them, I will again have compassion and will bring*

each of them back to his own inheritance and his own country.

And if they learn well the ways of My people and swear by

My name, saying, 'As surely as the Lord lives'—even as they

once taught My people to swear by Baal—then they will be

established among My people. But if any nation does not listen,

I will completely uproot and destroy it," declares the Lord.

Jeremiah 12:14–17

The Lord's demands were specific and concise. God was explaining that the nations had to (1) *encode, store,* and *retrieve* the behaviors of His people; (2) *encode, store,* and *retrieve* the importance of *His* name; and (3) acknowledge that He lives, in order to retrieve their inheritances. Notice that, although their own inheritance awaited them, damnation also awaited them. Whether they were established among God's people or experienced damnation depended on their willingness to learn accurate information.

Because thoughts generate behaviors, God was actually explaining that they had to learn a different way of thinking, a new culture. These nations had to believe in God and worship Him with their minds and spirits. Learning the ways of His people would have been the consequence of godly thinking. God was advising them to reject their negative thoughts, thoughts that caused their wicked behaviors.

When God explained that these nations must learn the ways of His people, He was actually saying they had to encode, store, and retrieve the power of His name. This means they had to learn *what* His name represents, learn *who* His name represents, learn who He is, and also learn *why* He exists.

Their obedience would have provided a relatively permanent change in their behaviors. From their learning, they would have had the opportunity to demonstrate new behaviors, behaviors they were unable to demonstrate prior to their learning. That is, their thinking would have transitioned from idolizing Baal to acknowledging and idolizing God, the Creator of the universe. This was God's purpose in requiring them to learn the ways of His people and to acknowledge Him. Their learning required observation, concentration, meditation, and repetition. These nations had to do whatever it took to store the name of the Lord in order to retrieve or to recall His true existence.

God places great emphasis on learning because learning opens the doors of success and failure. When you think of people you consider successful, what do you think they learned from experience that has led to their success today? Think about people you know who constantly experience failure. Do you think there is some information they are refusing to learn that is causing their continual failure?

Learning also leads to life and death. Although the enemy has tried on many occasions to take us out, many of us are still here today because of something we learned in our past. In the same way, many people are deceased today because of some behavior they learned at some point prior to their death.

Someone may say, "But what about grace? We are still here today because of grace." Yes, and my reply to this question is this: Those who are deceased because of some learned behavior also had access to grace. In fact, many who are deceased today honored God and lived through grace, but engaged in some behavior they learned and it resulted in their physical death.

THE MISCONCEPTION OF LEARNING

Many people have misconceptions of learning. One might say they have learned, but may not display learned behaviors. They may not show evidence of a change in their thoughts and actions. This is what the Lord was trying to get the nations who were plotting against Israel to realize. Evidently, the plotting nations encoded the wrong information prior to God's plan to uproot them. Prior to God's plans, their memory, learning, and knowledge reflected Baal. They worshipped Baal and despised God, based on behaviors they had learned. If they had encoded the wrong information about the true God because of their stubbornness and disobedience, or if they had not retained the information long enough, they would have eventually reverted to their original behaviors. This regression would have eventually destroyed them.

Understanding the demands God gave these nations is vital to our lives. If we don't encode, store, and retrieve the name of the Lord and acknowledge that "He surely lives," as God commanded the nations, we won't inherit the provisions He has awaiting us. And if we don't encode, store, and retrieve Christ's work at the cross, we will never develop spiritually. In the midst of our underdevelopment, we will continue to believe we must work for our salvation. We will not have true knowledge of grace. Consequently, we will believe that God desires to torment us because of negative behaviors, as opposed to learning that He is merciful about our sinful thinking and unrighteous living.

PSYCHOLOGICAL AND SPIRITUAL RESILIENCY

Having knowledge of Christ's work at the cross revitalizes our lives daily. No matter what state we are in, knowledge of the cross and believing in Christ's existence will keep us in perfect peace. Essentially, our peace depends on how we view godly information. The latter statement brings me to an important point. Just because we are living, does not necessarily mean we have life. In fact, many people are living, but are lifeless. Such people are living, but death is consuming them. You'll have to understand how I define life to appreciate this point.

I define life as *psychological resiliency* that is learned from knowing Christ is the ultimate provider. Based on my definition, life is a state of mind, just as success is a state of mind. I focus on our minds, because if they deteriorate, our being follows. It is important that you get this. Our being is through Christ, but how we use our minds determines our fate.

Psychological resiliency means having the ability to bounce back from misfortune; it means having the ability to live in the midst of pain, sorrow, and unhappiness. When you learn psychological resiliency through Christ's work at the cross, it doesn't matter if you look like death, feel like death, smell like death, and are surrounded by scavengers; your learned psychological resilience will keep death from consuming you.

This learned psychological state is what allows a speedy recovery from problems, whether the problems are personal, familial, financial, or societal. This knowledge teaches us that our living and being are through Christ. He created life, maintains life, and reestablishes life. Without His respiration, we are a stifling creation. At this moment, look inward and ask yourself these questions:

- Am I psychologically resilient?
- Do I have life?

Your psychological resilience is based on *listening* to and *learning* God's Word. Spiritual development is a consequence of encoding, storing, and retrieving His Word. Through encoding, storing, and retrieving God's Word, you will notice a relatively permanent change in your behaviors. But remember, your behavior change will be based on experience. If you continue to believe in Christ's work at the cross and retrieve the knowledge of grace on a daily basis, your behavior change will be rather stable. If you reject Christ's work at the cross and reject His grace and mercy, you will eventually forget what you had learned. Consequently, your daily problems will replace your memory for God's Word and you will place yourself at risk of losing your life (see the above definition of life). Remember, with Christ, you have life. If you reject Him and remove His Word from your memory, thoughts that lead to death will consume your mind.

ACCEPTING GOD'S INVITATION

It is extremely important that you understand the process of spiritual change that results from learning. The Bible explains that Jesus is the way, the truth, and the life (John 14:6, NKJV), but how does learning about this particular *way, truth,* and *life* affect our thinking in terms of psychological and spiritual change?

The process is as follows: Through His redemptive work on the cross, God has provided salvation for those who believe; by believing in Christ and accepting salvation, we become reborn mentally and spiritually; as a result of our rebirth we learn new information; from constant learning and adhering to this new information, God will gradually remove old, sinful habits from our mental processes; from gradually removing old information and allowing new information to govern our thoughts, we experience a *relatively permanent change in our behavior.* This is the entire process of renewing our minds. But remember, this change in behavior is based on experience and practice; it is based on abiding in Him and earnestly seeking His face and calling on His name. It is based on our ability to memorize, learn, and believe. The moment we disbelieve is the moment we place ourselves at risk for returning to our old, sinful mindset.

REBIRTH: THE SPIRITUAL CONSEQUENCE OF LEARNING

Now there was a man of the Pharisees named Nicodemus, a member of the Jewish ruling counsel. He came to Jesus at night and said, "Rabbi, we know you are a teacher who has come from God. For no one could perform the miraculous signs you are doing if God were not with him."

> *In reply Jesus declared, "I tell you the truth, no one can see the kingdom of God unless he is born again." "How can a man be born when he is old?" Nicodemus asked. "Surely he cannot enter a second time into his mother's womb to be born!" Jesus answered, "I tell you the truth, no one can enter the kingdom of God unless he is born of water and the Spirit. Flesh gives birth to flesh, but the Spirit gives birth to spirit. You should not be surprised at my saying, 'You must be born again.'*

John 3:1-7

As Jesus explained to Nicodemus, we must be born again. But being born again is a consequence of learning. Learning what the Bible says about daily living and believing in the Word are interventions that bridge the gap between carnality and spiritual development. Although Nicodemus was intelligent, his knowledge was full of worldly thinking, because he had no mental image of spirituality as it referred to being born again. Instead, he could only retrieve the concept of earthly impregnation concerning the rebirth.

> *"How can this be?" Nicodemus asked. "You are Israel's teacher,"*
> *said Jesus, "and do you not understand these things? I tell you*
> *the truth, we speak of what we know, and we testify to what*
> *we have seen, but still you people do not accept our testimony.*
> *I have spoken to you of earthly things and you do not believe;*
> *how then will you believe if I speak of heavenly things."*

John 3:9-12

One important question concerning this new life is, How do we allow our learning to be continual? The answer is we must continue to feed our minds and spirits with God's Word. Realize that our minds and spirits only lead to change; they do not create change. The Holy Spirit creates and dictates change.

How we use our minds determines our behavior change. Our experiences with God, through praise and worship, determine our intimacy with Him. Our minds and spirits must remain in harmony with God through learning about His true existence. This does not mean we are working for our salvation, but rather, we are working to understand the Person of Christ, through His work at the cross. It is impossible to appreciate an intimate relationship with someone we do not know.

I explained that our minds and spirits lead to change. This means if we decide that we no longer want grace to protect our minds and spirits, and we decide to return to our wicked ways, God's grace will allow this. God's grace will not throw us against the wall or pummel us until submission. Through God's grace, we have free will, and our will usually determines our destiny. It is through God's will that we align with His purpose. Success, both earthly and spiritually, is the product of God's will. But our free-will determines whether we'll submit to His will. This is why we determine our success.

If we do not feed our mind's spiritual nutrition, our behaviors will change relatively quickly given personal circumstances. Our faith will return to doubt. Since the mind and spirit lead to psychological and spiritual changes, which produce learning, many newly learned spiritual behaviors are forgotten relatively quickly. This is because our minds are often unequipped for spiritual warfare.

SPIRITUAL LEARNING: A CONTINUAL PROCESS

Refusing to learn of Christ's existence will inadequately prepare you for the trials and tribulations you will experience in life. Believers who attend church services, but do not engage in spiritual worship outside of church set themselves up for failure; they usually recreate sinful lifestyles, because they do not acquire the power to resist the devil. When nonbelievers convert to believers because of learning, Satan puts his game face on and rounds up his A-gaming demons to attempt to prevent the conversion. If new believers don't continue to feed their minds and spirits by continual learning of the Scriptures, they will not develop spiritually.

This is spiritual warfare. There is no way we can compete with demonic contenders with our limited strength. We must fuel our fire by preparing and strengthening our minds and spirits with the Word of God, and instead of taking on demonic forces head on, we must let God fight our battles.

I CONFESS: I TOO WAS HESITANT

If you are hesitant to give your life over to the Lord, I understand. I understand because I, too, was hesitant. But since I have totally dedicated my life to the Lord, I haven't been the same. The thoughts and behaviors that once characterized my life have been renewed. Now, I wake up in the morning energized to live a fulfilling life, a life pleasing to God.

If you are in disbelief, there is a good chance that you have not encoded and stored the wisdom of God that brings about retrieving blessings. I can make such a declaration, because I once resembled Nicodemus in my carnal thinking. I did not have the encoding knowledge and faith to retrieve the information that enabled freedom from my sinful mind. Don't allow Satan to accumulate questions that will delay your step; he did it to me, and for years I was a slave to his deception.

In Matthew 11:28-30, the Lord tells us what steps to take. Again, the steps are straightforward. He says to

> *[c]ome to Him, all who are weary and burdened, and He will*
> *provide rest. He says to take His yoke and learn from Him, for*
> *He is gentle and humble in heart, and you will find rest for*
> *your souls. He explained that His yoke is easy and His burden*
> *is light.*

When we learn of Christ, we encode, store, and connect our spirit with His Spirit. With this, we're able to retrieve His strength, faith, righteousness, and eventually, identity.

IMPORTANT SCRIPTURES TO ENCODE, STORE, AND RETRIEVE

At this moment, let's search the Scriptures for the purpose of learning about Christ. But remember, what we are about to cover is information within a text. We have to utilize the information by encoding and storing what we read and meditate on it to convert the information into a mental image:

> *That if you confess with your mouth, "Jesus is Lord," and*
> *believe with your heart that God raised Him from the dead,*
> *you will be saved. For it is with your heart that you believe and*
> *are justified, and it is with your mouth that you confess and*
> *are saved.*

> Romans 10:9

This is the foundation of salvation. As simple as the quotation: "If you confess with your mouth [Jesus is Lord] and believe in your heart that God raised Him [Jesus] from the dead, you will be saved." Even if you have no other understanding about Jesus Christ or the Bible, understanding this verse and believing—through faith—what the verse explains, you are saved. Now, develop your mind by reading His Word, and walk by faith, for your salvation is a faith walk.

Your spiritual life is a process. Your growth in the Lord comes through preparation—reading, praying, believing, and acting on God's Word—which brings about development. Spiritual development reflects learning, a process that brings about change. Use Romans 10:9 as a stepping-stone to your spiritual development. Once you confess with your mouth and believe in your heart, don't allow anyone to question your salvation. Don't let anyone tell you that you're not saved or that you have to engage in religious rituals to obtain God's salvation. Remember, salvation is a gift from God—you cannot earn it by performing religious works.

You are as saved as the believer who has been serving God for over 20 years. The believer who has been serving God for over 20 years also had to confess Romans 10:9 when they dedicated their life. However, they may have more knowledge in the Lord, because they have been encoding and storing biblical information throughout their development. But you and the person who has been saved for many years are receiving the same salvation, the salvation through Jesus Christ.

Congratulations, you have just earned everlasting life, upon your confession and belief. Now, your job is to strengthen and develop spiritually. Remember, Christ has saved you by grace. You are saved because you have confessed with your mouth and believed in your heart that God raised Jesus from the dead. Notice how confessing and believing are interdependent. You must confess and from confessing, you must learn to believe. Even if you don't have much knowledge concerning Christ and spirituality yet, your confession and willingness to learn are the seeds that will activate your faith.

But because of His great love for us, God, who is rich in mercy, made us alive with Christ even when we were dead in transgressions—it is by grace you have been saved.

Ephesians 2:4-5

For it is by grace you have been saved, through faith—and this not from yourselves, it is the gift of God—not by works, so that no one can boast.

Ephesians 2:8–9

For God so loved the world that He gave His one and only Son, that whoever believes in Him should not perish but have eternal life. For God did not send His Son into the world to condemn the world, but to save the world through Him. Whoever believes in Him is not condemned, but whoever does not believe stands condemned already because he has not believed in the name of God's one and only Son.

John 3:16–18

This righteousness from God comes through faith in Jesus Christ to all who believe. There is no difference, for all have sinned and fall short of the Glory of God, and are justified freely by His grace through the redemption that came by Christ Jesus. God presented Him as a sacrifice of atonement, through faith in His blood.

Romans 3:22-25

Notice the term *redemption.* This verse teaches us that when we sin and fall short of the Glory of God, we are indeed justified freely by grace through the redemption that came through Christ Jesus. In order to access redemptive works, we must repent. That is, we must train our minds—through faith in God's Word—to reflect the thoughts of Christ. Again, repentance means to change your mind. It is not simply verbalizing words in your head about how guilty and sorry you are for sinning against God. Repentance is the initial renewing process that leads to spiritual development. As defined in the *Random House College Dictionary,* the term redemption signifies the act of redeeming, delivering, and rescuing. Through repentance, God rescues us; when we allow Him to renew our minds, He delivers us from sinful lifestyles.

When the adversary comes to make you depressed or make you feel that you're not a believer, or make you believe that you are still in bondage, you have already been redeemed! God does not wait until we begin to face difficulties, and then start the process of redemption. Rather, God has already redeemed us. No matter how we fall, we have redemption through Christ.

The adversary does not want you to store this knowledge, because the information alone lets you know that God has already fought and won the battle for us. He has already defeated sin—all sin! However, I John verse 6 says, "No one who lives in Him keeps sinning. No one who continues to sin has either seen Him or known Him." This verse shows us that when we have Christ's Spirit, our minds begin to change such that our thinking and desires reflect His.

And we know that in all things God works for the good of those who love Him, who have been called according to His purpose. For those God foreknew He also predestined to be conformed to the likeness of His Son, that he might be the firstborn among many brothers. And those He predestined, He also called; those He called, He also justified; those He justified, He also glorified.

Romans 8:28–30

But not all the Israelites accepted the good news. For Isaiah says, "Lord, who has believed our message? Consequently, faith comes from hearing the message, and the message is heard through the word of Christ. But I ask: Did they not hear?"

Romans 10:16–18

TAKING THE POSITION OF GOD: HUMAN DEITIES

Understanding the information of Romans 8:28-30, why do we constantly ordain church folk to the ministry based on who we believe ought to teach or preach God's Word as opposed to allowing God's predestination to fulfill? God gave us natural, earthly abilities for a specific reason. He created us with the ability to procreate and commanded that we raise our children according to His will. We add to His command and will by predestining, confirming, justifying, and glorifying church folk according to self-righteous purposes.

Predestinating by self-will is why many believers are still in bondage. This is also the reason many man–made prophets are "practicing" in the church. It's no wonder you may have been lied to, in the form of a prophesy, on many occasions. You should not be surprised when the one you appointed, predestined, and glorified tells you a false prophesy, but says it's from the Lord.

If you are one who justifies church folk, are you aware that they are fallible? You must encode and store biblical knowledge so you can decipher spiritual pretenders. Not every prophetic word spoken in church is from God. Some words spoken actually seek to confine and victimize you. These words come from people who project their own thoughts and speak as if God is speaking through them. Ask God to give you the spirit of discernment so that you can become vigilant of these types of practices.

THE JOURNEY

We have discussed Bible verses that will permit everlasting life. As you know, you do not receive life because you have read the Scriptures. After you have read the Scriptures, confessed with your mouth and believed in your heart that Jesus is Lord, you are undeniably saved.

You have just jumped aboard, but caution: There will be many stops before your destination to attempt to make your ride uncomfortable. Do not get off before your designated location. Although things may seem glorious throughout the opening doors, do not exit because of temptations. Moreover, when the long ride appears to be unbearable, hold fast and retrieve the information you have stored through the Word of God. May God bless you. Buckle up with the Word, and enjoy your ride.

While riding,

Do your best to present yourself to God as one approved, a workman who does not need to be ashamed and who correctly handles the word of truth. Avoid godless chatter, because those who indulge in it will become more and more ungodly. Their teaching will spread like gangrene.

II Timothy 2:15–17

CHAPTER SUMMARY

In Jeremiah 12:14-17, God warned the many nations who were plotting to inherit the blessings He released to Israel. He explained that He would uproot them from their own lands. What I find most interesting is, although these nations were plotting to seize the inheritance of Israel, God was willing to establish them among His people. He was not going to establish them among His people without their own effort, however. Establishing them among His people was contingent on an important factor: whether they learned His people's ways. God based His decision solely on their ability to *learn!* Learning is important because, once we renew our minds, we must learn to think and behave as children of God.

REFLECTION AND DISCUSSION QUESTIONS:

- Jot down what you believe was most meaningful from this chapter—something that you will share with a friend or colleague.
- How is this chapter relevant to your experiences in life?
- What "aha" moments did you have while reading this chapter?
- Reflect on the story that I shared at the start of this chapter. Do you believe studying psychology is somehow contrary to Scripture?
- What is one thing you will change or reflect on more after having read this chapter?

SCRIPTURE TO REFLECT ON:
PROVERBS 9:9, NKJV

Give instruction to a wise man, and he will be wiser; Teach a just man, and he will increase in learning.

WHAT'S NEXT?

In the next chapter, I shed a light on why most believers are stagnated and unable to move forward to pursue their purpose. This stagnation is because we often ask God a three-letter word when He recommends that we do things. Learn why you must respond immediately when you hear the voice of God, and refuse to ask the three-letter word!

CHAPTER EIGHT:
God! Why Me?

Now when Herod saw Jesus, he was exceedingly glad; for he had desired for a long time to see Him, because he had heard many things about Him, and he hoped to see some miracle done by Him. Then he questioned Him with many words, but He answered him nothing.

Luke 23:8-9, NKJV

Throughout my natural and spiritual development, I often wondered why God gives commands without thoroughly explaining why each command is given. I also wondered why God emphasizes specific behaviors without explaining why we should engage in such behaviors. I often questioned why God required me to do certain things. In the process of my curiosity, I prolonged my calling. Instead of heeding God's call immediately, I adamantly asked the infamous question, "Why?"

Over time I have learned that we do not have to question God about His actions. I've learned that every command given is for the betterment of our earthly selves and spiritual development. I have also learned that after we follow God's instructions, the manifestation of His call will reveal His purpose, and the question *why* will be dismissed from our thoughts.

I understand that individuals who have recently accepted Christ as their Savior have questions. Asking why because you desire to understand spiritual development is appropriate and natural. Curiosity is normal. Asking questions and receiving feedback provide a sense of knowing. Asking questions and pondering specific concerns are very necessary if someone tells you to do something that appears to be life threatening, or simply unusual. However, we must learn that sometimes asking many questions about why we should commit to God's call may prolong our calling and hinder our development.

Asking questions is perfectly fine if these questions do not cause us to procrastinate or second-guess our willingness to develop spiritually. But we must understand that when we ask many questions, we often explain to ourselves why we shouldn't pursue specific objectives. We often become fearful, and when we do, we transition from living by faith to living by human abilities. We begin to focus on our inabilities and, thus, continue to question God. The act of questioning specific activities that occur in our earthly lives is imperative, but questioning the call of God will separate us from our purpose. When being advised about strengthening our earthly and spiritual lives, let's make transitions and preparations, instead of allowing our inquiries and doubt to dissuade us. I'll illustrate this concept.

THE INFAMOUS QUESTION: GOD! WHY ME?

If I organized a not-for-profit seminary that focused on improving our earthly and spiritual existence in Christ, and invited people to attend, many believers would ask the question: Why do I need to attend? However, curious people would attend, and if I told the group to follow four steps for an entire year, without asking why, the majority of the group would probably be unsuccessful, because they would be too concerned with wanting to know why they are being told to follow such procedures.

I could be preparing them for earthly and spiritual blessings, but their questions and concerns about their preparation would become barriers to their success. This would delay their blessings and eventually cause them to miss out. For example, if I told the group to engage in the following procedures for approximately four days a week, for one year, but do not ask why, if obedient, the group would see astounding results the subsequent year.

- **Procedure 1:** Join a health club and work out faithfully. The membership does not have to be from *Lifetime Fitness,* but simply a health club or gym where you could do cardio and simple weight training. If a health club is not accessible, take time out of the day to exercise at home; walk around your community.

- **Procedure 2:** During your downtime, read books. Don't simply read books like novels, but read them for understanding. Look up words you are unfamiliar with and write them down. After reading, question the author's reasoning. Review the unfamiliar vocabulary words daily.

- **Procedure 3:** Go to Bible study, study the Bible at home, and pray for understanding of biblical information.

- **Procedure 4:** Now that you have possession of this book, do not simply read it and allow it to collect dust. Instead, read it daily, even if you are able to recite chapters.

Although the four steps appear to be time consuming, they could definitely fit perfectly into your day. How? Well, substitute the four steps with the nonproductive things you may engage in throughout a given day. Even if I offered a free membership, if Bible study were next door to their homes, and if I sent each member a free book in the mail, people would still be preoccupied with asking "why!"

THE MANIFESTATION

Although I didn't explain why the group should engage in the seminary procedures, if the group members were obedient to the instructions, they would notice the following changes:

- From working out, they would have a bodily change—less fat and more muscle. They would be stronger and healthier, and would have better endurance and blood circulation.

- From reading, the group would improve their critical thinking, analytical reasoning, reading comprehension, writing skills, and enhance vocabulary: a total improvement in their thinking and reasoning abilities.

- From going to Bible study, the group would notice a growth in understanding Christ's work at the cross, grace and salvation.

They would experience a cohesive growth in their spiritual knowledge.

- From reading this book daily, the group would understand mental processes according to how Christ planned for us to use them at the earthly realm, for spiritual development. Group members would learn how to experience success in every area of their life!

By simply asking you to work out, read books, including the Bible and this book, without asking why, look at the amazing results: Obedience systematically allowed your mind to conceptualize and form mental images for the betterment of your earthly and spiritual existence. From engaging in the behaviors for a prolonged period, your body and mind would have become familiar with the activities and you would have noticed a *relatively permanent change in your behaviors!* This is one definition of learning.

The above illustration is a perfect example of the communion God shared with Adam, with the exception of asking *why?*

LEARNING HOW TO WORK IN CONGRUENCE WITH GOD

The Lord God said, "It is not good for the man to be alone. I will make a helper suitable for him." Now the Lord God had formed out of the ground all the beasts of the field and all the birds of the air. He brought them to the man to see what he would name them; and whatever the man called each living creature, that was its name. So the man gave names to all the livestock, the birds of the air and all the beasts of the field. But for Adam no suitable helper was found. So the Lord God caused the man to fall into a deep sleep; and while he was sleeping, He took one of the man's ribs and closed up the place

with flesh. Then the Lord God made a woman from the rib He
had taken out of the man, and He brought her to the man. The
man said, "This is now bone of my bones and flesh of my flesh;
she shall be called 'woman,' for she was taken out of man."

Genesis 2:18-23

In Genesis 2:18-23, Adam's life was characterized by complete harmony and compliance to God. Genesis did not record Adam asking God *why* he had to name the livestock, birds, wild animals, and the woman. When God brought His creation for Adam to name, can you imagine Adam saying, "God! Why me?" or, "God, you're going to have to give me a day or so to see if I'm feeling up to naming all this life you're bringing me!"

Wouldn't it be amazing if Genesis recorded such behaviors? Why would it be amazing if Adam approached God in this manner, but it isn't amazing to hear *whys* and *who-mes* from modern believers? Unlike our behaviors nowadays, Adam obeyed God's call immediately. Consequently, he was blessed beyond measure. Obedience opens the door to our destiny, God's will. Are you asking God "why me?" Or are you walking in His divine will?

Does the Lord delight in burnt offerings and sacrifices as much
as in obeying the voice of the Lord? To obey is better than
sacrifice.

I Samuel 15:22

DOES GOD OWE YOU?

The Lord commands us to demonstrate specific behaviors for the purpose of encoding and storing into our memory. He does this so we could eventually retrieve information that enables us to break through daily circumstances. For example, apply the previous seminary scenario to God and obedience. Many of us have a tendency to ask questions when God leads us to specific objectives, but when we retrieve blessings, the question *why* is never voiced. We always seem to understand why God blessed us, and we attribute the blessing to something that we did to earn it.

This understanding comes from the belief that God owes us blessings based on our good deeds. When we retrieve blessings, we tend to remember that we spent five minutes praying for a blessing and two minutes reading the Word. We automatically remember the two hours we took out of our Sunday to attend church, and the day we drove Brother John to the store.

Because of these works, we believe God is proud of our behaviors, so He sent a blessing in the mail. We must understand when God is speaking to us and we must refuse to question His reasoning and authority. When the Lord tells us to do something, there should be no misunderstanding. Usually, we misunderstand when we are not ready to submit ourselves to His call. We often act as if God has made a mistake and called upon the wrong person.

Our behaviors usually reflect the following thought: "Who? Me? God, are you sure you want me to?" The only time we should question the spirit is if it is another spirit other than God speaking. But the question still remains: If we don't encode and store the commands of God, how would we be able to retrieve and decipher who is commanding our behaviors? Likewise, how would we understand if the Spirit of God is speaking to us if we are unable to retrieve the Holy Spirit's voice, which is God's Word?

The irony in today's churches is many believers testify and explain that the Spirit of God is speaking to them, but these believers also admit that they seldom have time to study the Bible and pray outside of church. God manifests Himself and His voice throughout the Scriptures, but we must understand the language of faith in order to interpret His speech.

LEARNING OBEDIENCE AND COMPLIANCE

We must renew our minds by totally submitting and complying with the will of God by utilizing our ability to learn. We make the Lord's instructions more difficult than they actually are because we refuse to learn the ways in which He functions and manifests blessings. He may tell us to take one step; in response to His voice, we may take three steps. He may tell us to walk patiently and don't worry; in response to His voice, we may run a mile, get tired, stop, sit down, and contemplate our problems.

The Lord does not provide drawn out, difficult explanations of what we should do. Sometimes, He doesn't tell us in great detail why to do certain things. At other times, He may not tell us anything at all other than trust Him, have faith that His orders are purposeful, and worship Him throughout the process. And the fact is, this speech may not always come to you through some prophesy or dream, but you can always find it in His Word. This means, if we do not seek His voice through His Word, we may never hear from God. We are often preoccupied with wanting to hear prophetic words from prophets; at other times, we are preoccupied with wanting the prophet to share some divine revelation. But God is not that difficult. He doesn't only speak through prophets at revivals. He will speak to you through His Word! This means, you can have your own revival, in your own home, and hear from God daily.

THE INVITATION: YOUR OPPORTUNITY TO HEED THE CALL OF GOD WITHOUT ASKING "WHY?"

Here is a test of your obedience—a Scripture we previously visited:

> *Come to Me [come to God], all you who are weary and burdened, and I will give you rest. Take My yoke upon you and learn from Me, for I am gentle and humble in heart, and you will find rest for your souls. For My yoke is easy and My burden is light.*

> Matthew 11:28–30

This is your invitation to God, from God. At this moment, He is advising you to take upon His yoke and learn from Him. Like any invitation, you do not have to accept it if you do not desire. If you don't want to learn from Him and follow Him, what is so significant that is holding you back? What types of baggage are you carrying that will not allow you to take a step forward to Christ?

Give your baggage to the Lord, for you have been carrying it far too long. Because you have accepted Christ's invitation, your journey of depression, worry, and sorrow are a manifestation away from being defeated. You have arrived at your destination. Let the Lord levitate your spirit through His glory. Focus your mind on God's grace. Study His Word and become familiar with what He has promised you. Congratulations my friend. Enjoy your inheritance in Christ, and apply what you have learned to experience success in every area of your life!

CHAPTER SUMMARY

Throughout my development, I often wondered why God required us to demonstrate certain behaviors. Instead of heeding the call of God and responding to His voice immediately, I would constantly ask "why?" Because I was consumed with questioning God's directives and wondering why—instead of heeding his call immediately—I delayed my purpose and call in life.

Most people resemble me in that they are overly consumed with asking God why. Why, why, why, why? I have learned that we do not have to question God about His actions. I've learned that every command given is for the betterment of our earthly self and spiritual development. I have also learned that after we follow God's instructions, the manifestation of His call will reveal His purpose, and the question *why* will be dismissed from our thoughts. That is, when our purpose is revealed, from heeding the call of God, we will understand why He commanded us to engage in certain behaviors. Take a moment to reflect: Are you asking God "why me?" Or are you walking in His divine will?

REFLECTIONS AND DISCUSSION QUESTIONS:

- Jot down what you believe was most meaningful from this chapter—something that you will share with a friend or colleague.
- How is this chapter relevant to your experiences in life?
- What "aha" moments did you have while reading this chapter?
- Reflect on my experiences with questioning God?
- Have you been prolonging your calling by constantly asking God "Why me?"
- Why do you believe some people ask "Why me?" when God gives them a directive?
- What is one thing you will change or reflect on more after having read this chapter?

SCRIPTURE TO REFLECT ON:
I SAMUEL 15:22

Does the Lord delight in burnt offerings and sacrifices as much as in obeying the voice of the Lord? To obey is better than sacrifice.

WHAT'S NEXT?

This chapter is the final chapter of the book. Congratulations to you if you have read the entire book! I am an avid reader and writer at heart. When I read an entire book, one that is full of nuggets and recommendations on how to develop in different areas of life, I am overtaken with joy. It is an accomplishment for me. I take great pride in studying to improve all areas of my life. With this, if you have completed this book, then you should feel elated! You should have the tools to develop spiritually and achieve the blessings that God has for you.

So *what's next?* Well, as you know, there are no more chapters. But the concepts of this book should be in your mind. It was Oliver Wendell Homes Jr. who said, "A mind that is stretched by new experiences will never be satisfied with going back to its old dimensions." I am confident that the content of this book has stretched your mind.

I am confident that you no longer want to go back to depending on success the world's way. I am confident that you do not want to live a life apart from God. So what's next? Application! Applying what you have learned to bring heaven to Earth is next. Be sure to reflect on the chapter questions to identify how much you have grown. It was a pleasure working with you throughout the pages of this book. Be sure to contact me with your thoughts, concerns, and ideas.

Until the next book is released . . .

REFERENCES

Diller, J. V. (2007). *Cultural diversity* (3rd ed.). Belmont, CA: Thomsom Brooks/Cole.

Merriam-Webster's collegiate dictionary (10th ed.). (2002).

Prince, J. (2010). *Unmerited favor.* Lake Mary, FL: Charisma House.

Sternberg, R. J. (2003). *Cognitive psychology* (3rd ed.). Belmont, CA: Wadsworth.

The random house college dictionary (first ed.). (1975). New York, NY: Random House, Inc.